The Power and the Glory

The Power and the Glory

Arthur White

and Martin Saunders

Authentic

LONDON ● COLORADO SPRINGS ● HYDERABAD

This book is dedicated to the two most precious gifts ever given to me . . . my daughter and son, Emma and James. I love you both so much.

Dad

Contents

Ten Years Later . . .

Outside the thick, grey prison walls, it was -35°. Shivering, I approached the old gymnasium with a rhino-necked guard on either side of me. From within, the blood-curdling shouts of every kind of violent criminal reverberated, getting louder with each step. As I tried fruitlessly to decipher their words, I wondered how I'd managed to end up here, in this near-forgotten corner of a once-mighty Russia.

I hadn't hurt anyone here. I hadn't killed anyone. When they finally got me into a prison, it wasn't due to any offence committed on Russian soil. It was much more complicated than that. The sum total of more than twenty years of violence, filth and fury had put me in this place. They'd brought me here because of everything I'd ever done.

One of the rhinos unbolted the heavy metal doors to the gymnasium and swung them open. I felt a hand press firmly in my back, and I walked through. With the arctic temperatures outside, the prison wardens had improvised a heating mechanism. They were directing the exhaust from a big old generating set, which was running outside, through the window and into the hall. So while I could hear the inmates, I couldn't see them too well; the air was thick with smoke. The health and safety regulations in Russian prisons do not exactly lead the world. What I did see, emerging from the cloud, was a six foot, bare-chested Goliath with a fixed sneer. He beat his muscular chest; this, I was informed, was to be my opponent.

When I first arrived in Russia, I'd spent a few nights in a young offenders' institution before they'd been able to transfer me. I noticed that the younger prisoners there all had fat, swollen hands; apparently they inject Vaseline into their fingers to make them swell up. When I asked why, I was told that they did it to improve their fighting ability – to give them firmer, heavier fists that could cause more damage. At night, they sleep in dormitories, not cells, and once the guard locks the door it's survival of the fittest. So the Vaseline, that's just the way they survive. I could understand that. Right now I could see that Goliath had those same, tellingly thick fingers. He'd spent his life building his body – it was probably all he'd ever done since he was a boy.

The gym building, as with the rest of this and most other Russian prisons, was imperfectly preserved: still pretty much as it was when it was built in 1945. The smoke cleared enough for me to make out an iron balcony around the top of the room, full of prisoners, all with shaved heads and dressed in grey. Up there, and at my level, there were what seemed like a hundred guards.

The big Russian lump strode towards me and grinned. He was sure he'd have the beating of an old boy like me. But he didn't know me nearly well enough to go making assumptions like that.

1

Invincible

I'm a world champion. Four times over. My sport, powerlifting, is a close relative of weightlifting, but with different lifts. It's all about brute strength: the ability to lift and raise huge amounts of weight in the heat of competition. Like I said, I'm four times a World Champion. I've also won the European title six times, and the British nine. Not that I'm counting or anything.

There are three disciplines in powerlifting: the bench press, where you lie on a horizontal bench and try to push a weight upwards with your arms; the squat, where you carry a bar of weights on your shoulders, you squat down and try to come up again; and the dead lift. That one's my speciality. It's the simplest event in powerlifting, and the one that involves the most weight – the ultimate test of raw strength. With the dead lift, it's just you and the bar. All you've got to do is pick it up, hold it for a few seconds, and lower it to the floor. Which would be a lot easier if it didn't weigh the same as a small car.

I once lifted 382.5 kg. That's a lot of weight. I trained for most of my life to be able to do things like that. And just like many of the other things I've done in my life, powerlifting nearly got me killed.

I've had a lot of fights in my years. My fists might not be pumped full of Vaseline, but they still bear the scars of war. The first fight I can remember was when I was in the first year of senior school, with this guy from the other side of our estate called Charlie Hill (that's the name of the kid, not the estate). We had a lot in common: I was twelve years old, and I was one of the biggest kids in my year; so was Charlie. He was the hard nut from his side of the estate and I was the little hard nut from my side. I was the bigger of the two, because I was quite a big boy – I was six foot and half an inch at fifteen and then I stopped growing. By comparison, he was a little ginger fella, but even at that age he was the sort of bloke you didn't want to mix it with, full of fire.

We had a fight in the cloakroom. He didn't beat me but I didn't beat him, and we ended up standing off each other, snarling with a kind of mutual respect. I remember standing there, facing up to this little ginger kid with both our blood on the floor. He had a bloody nose and I had a puffy eye, or it might have been the other way around. We left the fight there though: the spoils were shared and we ended up being friends, although never close ones. That was how it worked, even in the playgrounds of East London – the culture was all about earning one another's respect.

While I never took my fighting skills into the boxing ring, I was a good all-round sportsman at school, and that elevated me socially. (Ever notice how the kids in the football team never get bullied?) I could run, play football and cricket, and I was popular partly as a result of that. If a prize was given for sport, Arthur White got it. And even though the stereotype would tell you that I wouldn't have been very academic, that's not exactly true – I got prizes for that, too, and I was pretty good at reading and writing. With all that success came a bit of credibility. I was always involved if a fight was going on, so I got the feeling I was pretty tough; I was excelling on the sports pitch and in the classroom throughout my schooldays. It got me feeling pretty good about myself, and when the teachers didn't know about the fights I'd been in, I expect they'd have described me as a model pupil.

Now, while I was involved in a fair few fights, I have to say at this point that, in my defence, I was never a bully. In fact, I'd often fight for someone else's cause rather than my own. I would often get dragged up to the headmaster after I'd had a fight protecting Reg Clark, because he was the biggest wimp on two legs and everybody picked on him. Tony Warner was the class bully, and when he bullied Reg, which he frequently did, I'd bash Tony and end up in the head's office.

The problem was, I had a strong sense of justice back then. If someone called me off to help them in a fight, I'd usually go even though it had nothing to do with me, just to help out a friend in trouble. I had more mates who were geeks than were sportsmen, because they knew that if they befriended me, I'd protect them. I didn't get paid for it – I just had this sense of righteousness about me that made me want to stick up for the underdog. I felt that I had quite a privileged position, being so popular, sporty, academic and hard. So I used my power to help people. Despite my frequent fighting appearances, I'd say I was a pretty decent bloke at school, and I think most of my classmates would have agreed.

I spent my teenage years living in a big housing estate in Loughton, Essex. It's the part of the world where the sprawl of East London finally comes to an end, and even being on an urban estate, there were acres of open space nearby as we bordered the beauty of Epping Forest. As a boy, I would love to go walking through fields not far from my house where I'd find myself chest-deep in corn. It was all so different to the place where I grew up as a young child – 1950s London, a place that was still badly scarred by the then recent onslaught of war. Here it was peaceful, and we were very happy as a family there.

My dad was a firm but fair man, and a traditional head of the household. He was a hard-working sort and a strong role model, although we weren't close – at least not during my childhood. I was much closer to my mum, like any good East End lad, and it was with her that I would talk about emotions and feelings.

Between the ages of fourteen and sixteen, I became more heavily involved in competitive sport, although not using my fists. As I said, I was an all-rounder, but my speciality above all others was sprinting. Mr Sethers, the gym master at my school, invited those in my class who were interested in representing the school in athletics to attend an after-school trial. I was excited to get the opportunity to prove myself, and that's exactly what I did. Sethers was impressed by my speed and strength and encouraged me to really strive and develop in the sport. I think I was probably born with a competitive

spirit and desire to succeed, but his mentoring certainly helped me to focus and channel my energies.
Under Sethers's guidance, I won a series of titles for
my school and myself, including Essex Junior
Champion. By the time I was sixteen, I'd already
equalled the British 100 metres record for my age.

Perhaps I could have gone on to be a champion
sprinter, but before that could happen, a much
greater passion got in the way. At that age, I started
to go to the gym to work out. A lot of my friends did
the same, and I enjoyed the challenge of improving
my body and lifting bigger, heavier weights. Even
then, people told me I was naturally strong, that I
had a real potential for lifting the really big weights.
Weightlifting became my new focus, and having
ascended to the top of sprinting in my area, I quickly
discarded that sport for this new one, which I found
far more exciting.

Of course, working out isn't always the most
thrilling pastime – quite often it's monotonous, and
sometimes it's pretty painful. But the gyms themselves – and I'm not talking about your local health
club here – were always a great source of entertain-
ment and full of characters, and that made them
addictive. Most of London's hardest men could be
found in these gyms – that was one of the ways they
kept up their strength, and their image.

I even met one of the world's most famous men in one of these places. Later, when I was about nineteen, I was training in a gym in Forest Gate owned by a man named Wag Bennett. Wag knew this Austrian bodybuilder, who came over to stay with him when the amateur Mr Universe competition was being held in the UK. His name was Arnold Schwarzenegger.

One time, he came down to the gym for a photo shoot and went to get changed in the lean-to at the back of the gym. It was a tight space, and he was obviously a big young man. When he put his arm up to get his shirt off, his fist went straight through the plastic roof! He wasn't big compared to some today, but he had a classically strong physique, and he was probably the best bodybuilder of his time. He used to come to the gym quite regularly to train with us, and we'd talk as best we could. At that time of course, he didn't have much English, but he was a great bloke, and I liked him a lot. Had Wag not persuaded him to go to America (in a way, Wag is indirectly responsible for *The Terminator*!), I'm sure I would have seen a lot more of him.

A lot of the foundations for my later life were laid in those teenage years. As well as developing a winning mentality, learning how to succeed as a sportsman and discovering the strenuous joys of weightlifting, I also met and fell in love with the girl who would go on to become my wife. Jacqui and I met when we were both fourteen. I was sitting on the wall of a pub – The Gunmakers' in Loughton – when she strolled by. I'll never forget the moment I first laid eyes on her – it was a lightning-bolt moment and love at first sight. We'd only been going out for a few days when I realised that this was the girl I wanted to marry, and while the law forced me to wait a few years for that privilege, my instincts were proved absolutely right. We married in 1971 – aged nineteen.

I left school three years before that. At seventeen I joined a building firm as an apprentice carpenter and joiner. C.S. Foster & Sons was a great firm to work for, and I threw myself into the job, unafraid of some honest hard work and enjoying my role as the youngest member of staff. The older blokes took me under their wing and were happy to show me the ropes. In turn, I worked hard for them, and would regularly come home with my hands bleeding because I wouldn't put the hammer down until a job was done, even when I blistered and bled (I still can't soften my hands up today). I grew up quickly, learning my trade and how to be a man from the older tradesmen at the company.

In 1972, I took the decision to leave the company and go self-employed. I'd learned my trade fully, and liked the idea of being my own boss – however much I'd enjoyed working at C.S. Foster & Sons. I was married, I was successful and I was strong. I felt like I had truly become a man, and as such disliked the idea of working for anyone else. I didn't see that as arrogant; I was simply an ambitious and confident person and saw no reason why I shouldn't work on my terms, with the skills that I had acquired.

The early years of my marriage were very happy. Not once since the day I met her had my eyes ever deviated from Jacqui; she was beautiful, my best friend and all I'd ever wanted from a woman. When I was working on building sites with big groups of blokes, I would often turn away when they wolf-whistled at a pretty passing girl in a miniskirt. It didn't interest me to even think about other women – it just wasn't on my radar. With my business, my sport and my happy marriage, life was sweet and happy. I had no reason to wish for any more.

My body was shaping up nicely. I used to spend hours in front of the mirrored walls of Wag Bennett's gym, just admiring myself, and in particular my bulging muscles. But the strength that I had wasn't limited to superficial muscle. The guys at the gym explained that I had tendon strength, which is something some people are just born with, and also a big strong skeletal frame. It was this threefold package of strengths that set me apart as a potential world class powerlifter. A lot of the blokes in the gym could see that, even in my early twenties.

In 1977, I ventured further into the business world by buying into a haulage company called L.G. Pearce. Lenny Pearce, the founder, had a heart attack and decided to find a buyer, which turned out to be me, my brother-in-law and a woman named Helen. She was a girlfriend of another business associate, a builder. Through her, he put a bit of money into our business, basically so that his bit-on-the-side had something to do.

We had six tipper lorries that we used primarily to take rubbish away from building sites and site clearances. We also had a contract with Readymix Concrete over at Hertford, where they used us to move sand around. Readymix had an enormous sand pit over there, where they would excavate sand and make it into concrete. The quarry itself was huge, going on for miles. They would dredge it from one end and load up our lorries, then we would run the sand along their land and tip it at their plant, where it went into the mixers to make concrete. We had three lorries over there doing this. As the demands of the contract increased, we ended up moving all our small (10-tonne) lorries over there, and getting rid of the two larger ones that we'd been using for site clearances.

We had four lorries over there, and because the work was being done on private land, we didn't need to tax, insure or MOT them. Everything was going well, and we were making an awful lot of money from this relatively simple contract: all the drivers had to do was drive backwards and forwards. My brother-in-law, Terry, understood the mechanics, so he looked after the maintenance of the lorries. I'd occasionally get a phone call from the plant saying one of the lorries had let them down and I'd have to go over to see Terry and get him to sort it out.

Eventually, we got more and more complaints. I went over there to try to sort things out, and the lorries looked like they'd been through a war. Doors were hanging off, tyres were shredded. It seemed that the drivers, bored by this monotonous driving task, had taken to racing each other across the pit in these trucks, or running their own time trial competitions to see who could do a run in the fastest time. Even though we didn't have to maintain the lorries to roadworthy standards, they still had to run, and the drivers had run them into the ground. Horrified by the death of my cash cow, I had to go to the office and tell the company they'd have to get another contractor in.

That was the end of L.G. Pearce, which had been a well-known name in local industry for a number of years. But I still had the lorries! Four massive 10-tonne trucks that could barely drive in a straight line. They weren't MOTd and never would be – they were completely useless. I didn't fancy parking them in my garden, so I came up with an idea. At the far end of the Readymix site, there were the giant sand pits that they couldn't mine any more, and which were now filled with water. They were very deep – certainly deep enough to hide a few lorries. When no one was around, I drove each truck to the edge of the pit, left the engine running and stepped out just in time, sending the trucks hurtling down to a watery grave. A few years later, during a particularly hot summer, I was driving past the old pits, which were now being used as landfill sites. I couldn't believe my eyes – the roofs of the lorries were sticking out of the water! I drove on quickly, and prayed I hadn't left anything incriminating in there. I couldn't help laughing, though.

By my late twenties, I don't think I'd changed much from when I was a kid. I still had that champion mentality; still had that burning sense of justice. I was generally well liked and respected within the trade, among my friends, and around the gyms that I'd frequent. Pretty much everything I'd touched went my way. I chose the woman I wanted, and she willingly married me. I made my own decisions in the world of work, and they all came off. I was still that great sportsman, who won more often than he lost. I had a lot of success, and not a lot of failure in my life. I also had the biggest muscles of anyone I knew of my age.

That led to me having a very high opinion of myself indeed. It wasn't arrogance, I didn't walk around telling people how great and strong I was, it was something else. When I daydreamed, I fantasised about performing superhuman feats in impossible situations. I imagined that I'd be caught in a train wreck but emerge unscathed, helping survivors out of the wreckage by literally hoisting the carriages in the air like a human crane. Or I'd be involved in a terrible car accident and have my body skewered by a huge piece of metal. When the rescue teams arrived, I'd simply pull the metal out of my chest and walk away.

I thought I was invincible.

2

Cracks in the Ice

At the beginning of the 1980s, Jacqui and I were living in Loughton, where we've lived all our lives. We had a nice house and to make it even nicer I bought the house next door and knocked it through. We had a big living space and plenty of money. We also had two children – Emma, who was born in 1977, and James, who came along three years later. I had a good construction business going, with contracts with the local councils for maintenance on schools, and also some private contracts. So everything in my life was continuing to go very well. I'd also begun to lift competitively, and had some excellent early results.

When I'd started doing weight training aged fourteen, it was only as an aid to sport fitness. That all changed when I met a guy at our local youth centre called Johnny Morris. Johnny was a bodybuilder and a good one – he'd managed to come second in the Mr Universe competition one year, and he got me into serious training. He was the one who introduced me to Wag Bennett's gym in Romford, and to some of the weightlifters there. One of them was called George Manners, and he told me that he was one of the coaches at the Bethnal Green Weightlifting Club, which was nearby. After a few months, he came over to me and told me he'd been watching me in the gym and thought I could be something special. He invited me to come to his club, and partly due to the feeling of flattery, I agreed.

Going along to Bethnal Green Weightlifting Club always gave me a special feeling – I loved it there. A lot of my family came from the East End of London, so in a sense I felt like I was getting back to my roots. In a strange way, training with the guys there was like being with family – and George took on the role of father figure. George was a former Olympic weightlifter, having competed in the 1964 Olympics and won countless other competitions. He was a great guy but a disciplinarian who worked us hard, and I learned a tremendous amount from him.

In 1975, George encouraged me to become a weightlifting instructor. Since he was my mentor, and I pretty much did whatever he told me to, I agreed to go on the relevant course. It was being held at the British National Sports Centre, at Bisham Abbey in Oxfordshire. On the course I met this guy called Ron Reeves, who ran a gym in Sittingbourne, and who worked with powerlifters as well as weightlifters. One day, I was dead lifting and he came over to me.

'Do you know what you're training with there, son?' he asked in his gravelly voice.

What I didn't realise was that the weight I was lifting – fairly comfortably – was very close to the then-British record. With Ron standing there, I attempted the British record and, to his astonishment, lifted it. From his expression, and the applause all round, I realised that I was actually quite good at this. Still hungry to be the best I could be in all areas of my life, I immediately switched all of my focus from weightlifting to powerlifting. Ron had a proposal for me, too: he had a team of power-lifters who com-peted at the weekends, and he wanted me to join it. I hadn't got into lifting in order to enter competitions – George had been steering me towards instructing – but something flared up in me and I jumped at the chance. I was still the same Arthur White from school who couldn't resist the chance to compete and win.

Within six months of making the switch to power-lifting in 1976, I'd qualified for the British

Championships, and broken the British and European records in the dead lift. At the British Championships in 1977, I even had the audacity to attempt the world record, which I almost got. Standing alongside all these other lifters who'd lived and breathed the sport since they were young, here I was competing well, and I'd just drifted into it through general weight training. It just came naturally to me.

When Emma was born, just after those championships, I couldn't have been more delighted. My business career was flying (at that stage, the L.G. Pearce lorries were still functional and raking in the Readymix money), my love of sport had developed into a very promising international career, and my marriage was not only rock solid but had produced a wonderful daughter. As a baby, she was an absolute angel from day one. From the day she came home, she slept long and deep – we even had to wake her up at night to feed her!

Well, if she was the perfect baby, then her brother was unfortunately the exact opposite of that. Having had Emma as my only first-hand experience of a baby, the arrival of James was like getting hit by a 14 lb sledgehammer. Whereas his sister was meek, gentle, quiet and a frequent sleeper, James barely slept a wink. He was an absolute nightmare, crying night after night. It was horrible. It was obvious to Jacqui that something wasn't right with him, and for several years after his birth we found ourselves going backwards and forwards to the doctor. For years, he wasn't sleeping. And I mean years; it was really bad. On one of these trips, the doctor said that James had very bad tonsils, which were giving him very bad sore throats, and could explain his constant discomfort. The NHS wouldn't operate, but this doctor said that James should have his tonsils out, even at three years of age. We took out private insurance and got him booked in privately. We took him into the hospital on a Sunday.

I took James and his mum to the hospital, dropped them off, and came home, as I had to look after Emma. Then, just a couple of hours later, I got a phone call from Jacqui asking me to return to the hospital. When I got there, a nurse explained that they had gone through their regular pre-op tests, and they'd found blood in his urine, which indicated a major problem. They did further examinations, and found out that James – my poor little three-year-old – had kidney stones. And not just that; these were the most enormous stones that any of the doctors had ever seen or heard of in a child of his age. They were literally as big as a hat – there was no way he was ever going to pass them. Even an adult couldn't have done so.

After exhaustive tests, they found that the kidney on his right side wasn't functioning properly, so there was talk of taking it out. His urethra tube was deformed, and they were talking of taking that out, too. Obviously, his bladder was also affected. So when they did operate, it was a massive piece of surgery, especially for such a small boy. It left a huge scar, running from the middle of his chest to the middle of his back – and that was only the first operation.

He'd been in hospital for about a month when suddenly things turned very grave. I got a phone call one night from a doctor telling me that James's temperature was rising, beyond anything that they could control. It was so bad that they were literally packing him in ice. And then the doctor spoke a handful of awful words – one of the worst sentences a father can hear: 'I'm afraid it's possible that we could lose him.'

I was in the car in a matter of seconds and drove at breakneck speed to get to the hospital as quickly as physically possible. It was the one thing I thought I could do to help; being a man who was so used to having control, this situation was completely desperate, and I felt particularly helpless. I almost couldn't cope, and as I swerved around the Essex roads, tears rolled down my cheeks. I cried out – to

God or whoever – begging that my son wouldn't die.

I burst into the room and Jacqui, who had been with him all the time, looked up at me with tears in her eyes. It was all still very much in the balance. Then, as time was running out for James, one of the team of doctors gave him an aspirin suppository – a relatively simple measure considering the life-or-death circumstances. And, as Jacqui and I held tightly onto one another and gazed down at the little boy who might be taken from us at any moment, something incredible happened. Purely thanks to the aspirin, James's temperature suddenly began to fall. Within minutes, it was at almost normal levels. The doctors were shocked that such a small intervention had made such a huge improvement. Having been there, I can only explain it as a miracle.

A few months later, James had to go back to the hospital for a final operation. They took his urethra tube and re-inserted it into his bladder. Thankfully, this was to be his final piece of major surgery, but if he had not had the operation, he would have certainly died. Because of his kidney stones, his urine was being siphoned backwards, and it would have just poisoned him. It's no exaggeration to say that there were many different points in the first three years of his life that James could have died.

So in all sorts of ways, James was a massive shock to my system. I'd been dragged out of the comfort zone that I'd been living in for more than a decade. Suddenly, here was something that wasn't going well, that wasn't easy and straightforward. And rightly or wrongly, my reaction was to retreat and run. When James was a small baby, his crying drove me absolutely insane. Again, here was something that I – the all-conquering Arthur White – had no way of controlling. So I started looking for excuses to get out of the house. I'd go to work early, at six in the morning, claiming that I had lots to do even when I didn't, because compared to the screaming madhouse I was leaving behind, work was a haven. Then at the end of the working day, I'd go straight to training and not get home until ten at night. I'd open the front door, and almost every day, Jacqui would be sitting at the top of the stairs, crying her eyes out, and James would be in his room screaming. We thought he was tired, or hungry, or simply needing pacifying – we didn't know that he was in pain from all the stuff going on inside him. Screaming was the only way he knew how to communicate, and unfortunately, all screams sounded the same to me.

James's problems – and the way I dealt with them – put a lot of strain on my relationship with Jacqui.

The pattern of our weeks would see me out lifting and working, and Jacqui at home with the baby. Before long, our tight marital bond was beginning to loosen. We didn't drift far apart, but the cracks began to appear.

While my marriage and home life was declining, I escaped in powerlifting, and I was getting better and better at it by the day. As each championship went by, I was moving closer to the biggest prizes and records. Everyone was talking about me as a world beater, and the big lifters in my class were becoming increasingly worried about my potential. I was a bit frustrated though; I didn't like losing, even if I was finishing on the podium in second or third place. I did win a major tournament – the European Championships – in 1981, but my eyes were always on the biggest prize: World Champion. Spurred on by the difficulties in my family, I vowed to get even better, whatever the cost.

Lots of us were into supplements and proteins, but until 1982 I'd managed to keep it legal, without resorting to steroid use. I'd heard a lot about these illegal muscle-building drugs, but since the weightlifting fraternity that I trained with in Bethnal Green were very strict about not touching them, I steered clear. That changed once I started getting more fully involved with the British powerlifting team. Unlike the more established sport of weightlifting, powerlifting was still in its infancy in the UK at that time, and powerlifters from up and down the country were all using steroids. The sport simply hadn't grown up enough to boot the drug cheats out. It was funny though, because nobody would admit to using, even though everybody knew who was. They'd still deny it if you asked them – perhaps because they wanted to preserve the illusion that they were honest, or that all their immense strength came naturally. Once I realised how rife this drug abuse was, I became even more frustrated. Not only was I coming second or third, I was losing out to steroid abusers. Since I didn't fancy becoming a grass, I felt there was only one option left open to me: if I couldn't beat them, I'd join them.

At that time, I got to know a powerlifter from Devon called Jim Duncan. He was a country boy, and he used to be able to get hold of animal steroids very cheaply from a mate of his who was a vet. Although not intended for human consumption, these steroids are used openly by vets because they offer a simple method of treatment for a sick or injured animal. I got to be good mates with Jim, and he offered to get hold of some of these steroids for me from his mate.

I hadn't really touched drugs too much, although they were always floating around the gym and the weightlifting scenes in general. My first experience of performance-enhancing substances was when I was lifting in the 1980 World Championships. I was in bronze position, having lifted 360 kg, but I was frustrated, knowing that to win the world title I would need to lift 410 kg or 903 lb. Nobody had ever lifted that much.

The world record was 395 kg, and it had been lifted on the same day by a guy called John Cook. I had a friend there named Mark, who would regularly import bags full of steroids into the country. He came up to me, and stuck a needle in my arm. It was a shot of adrenaline, which was legal, and from that point on I was pumped up with power. As I walked out to the lifting platform, I smashed the door off of its hinges, and when I got on to the stage I knocked a cameraman off of it. I attacked the bar, and even managed to get it up to my knees. I couldn't quite manage to straighten up and lock out, but for a few seconds as I tried, you could have heard a pin drop in that hall. It was then that, possibly subconsciously, I realised just what an effect drugs could have on me.

It all started quite slowly from there. Jim got me used to the steroids – which we referred to as 'the gear' – and they began working almost straight away. I could feel my body changing considerably, and I started taking a little more, and then a little more. Before I knew it, I was using very regularly.

There is a natural progression with any drug addiction: with alcohol, anti-depressants, even with steroids. At first, you just take something to give you a little bit of support, but then before you know it, you've started to become dependent. In one way, the transformation is slow, but in another way it's terrifyingly quick; it gets into your system like a smoking habit. Initially, the change I felt in my body was an increase of adrenaline. Jim must have pumped a lot into me because we'd use it in two ways at once: we used to open the sealed bottles and dilute the gear with orange juice, and sometimes we also took it intravenously, which hit the system a lot quicker. Adrenaline was the first rush or buzz I'd had from a drug, and it had two conflicting effects on my brain. I enjoyed the rush, and the heightened state it gave me which in turn helped me to lift bigger weights. At the same time, though, I was already searching for a bigger buzz. Again, going through Jim, I got hold of some ephedrine, which provided a bigger rush and was very common with lifters at that time. Very quickly, I'd even started to dabble with the occasional snort of cocaine, which gives you an instant hit. I would only take it before a competition or a massive training session, and so I wasn't too worried about it. I wasn't addicted and I was using these drugs to help me excel. And that's exactly what happened – I came second in the 1981 World Championship, and a few months later lifted my biggest ever total, in Germany.

Because of my size, weight and the huge physical exertion involved in what I was doing, the drugs would get used up very quickly by my body, and there were no discernible after-effects. And since I wasn't using them for anything other than as an aid to powerlifting, I didn't think I needed them any more than I decided to use them. Being a practical bloke and looking at things logically, I'd used them and I didn't need them any more, until the next time. At least, that's what I convinced myself of.

Underneath the surface, though, something was definitely going on, even if I had convinced myself that I was totally in control. I was taking more and more steroids, and trying every new type that came out. At that time in the early 1980s, I still wasn't into it half as heavily as most of the other blokes on the scene, but an addiction was slowly growing, and dangerously I was unaware of it. The hooks were in and my need was growing. Later, at some point in the mid-80s, I took a step across the line, and suddenly I was taking it every day. It was an easy step to make.

James recovered, and even began to sleep at night. More importantly, Jacqui began to get a full night's sleep after more than three years of torture. Emma was still an angel, and with her brother much more peaceful, we settled back into our happy family unit once more. Which was great – except that it meant that we didn't address any of our problems. We were so relieved to be sleeping again that we simply papered over the cracks. It didn't seem to be too much of a problem though, and it meant that I naturally spent more time around the house once more. To use a building analogy: our foundations had been rocked, but we were so happy that the house was still standing that we didn't bother to get the place checked out for structural damage. My foundations would be rocked again soon after.

When my dad left the army, he went to work for the Royal Corps of Commissionaires in London. It was established to find work for ex-servicemen such as him, and through their scheme he served as a messenger for a firm of stockbrokers. He had been working there happily for a good number of years, when one of his bosses, who was the chairman of the stock exchange, put his name forward to become a Freeman. This is an award, dating back to the thirteenth century, and it's a prestigious slice of London's cultural history. A Freeman of the City of London has certain bizarre rights, including the right to drive sheep and cattle over London Bridge! So it's only a nominal title, but it's used to honour good men and women of distinction.

It was a great honour for my dad to become a Freeman, purely for his services to the stockbrokers in the city. He even had his picture in the local newspapers. After he'd been given this honour, he then got approached by a few people who were Freemasons, which was common when someone became a Freeman. They wanted him to join their guild, and he accepted their offer. This was around 1983, two years prior to his death.

I had a good relationship with my father, especially as he got older. When he was made a Freemason, he retired from work because he had dodgy legs that were capable of getting him about but not up to the demands of a messenger job. Generally, his health was awful, especially as he got older. He suffered from bad arthritis; he had a number of serious heart attacks – probably about seven or eight in all, and a few of them were big ones. Like many men of his age, after the war he did little or no exercise, save for the walking he did at work, but he smoked heavily: he would probably smoke sixty a day. He drank quite heavily, too, and I remember that he would always have a drink, every day. My dad was a pest when he'd had a drink; he would fight the world. He was a bit of a hard nut, too, and he could handle himself. So as a drinker and smoker with a poor diet, whose only exercise came from walking and the occasional scrap, I guess you could say his whole lifestyle wasn't all that healthy. He was my dad, though, and I looked up to him and loved him.

When he packed up work as a messenger, he actually came to work for me part time. I used to take him down to the yard where I ran a construction business, and he used to make me tea, clean up the car and look after the yard for me. I'd give him a few quid, and it kept him from boredom and getting under my poor mum's feet. So we had a good relationship, and in fact for the first time we were getting to be quite friendly – as mates, rather than as father and son. I used to take the mickey out of him for being a Freemason, because he used to have a little Freemason's Bible, which he would study day and night. It was a proper little leather-bound book, just the size and shape of one of those tiny New Testaments. It wasn't a proper Bible of course – it told you all the things that you have to remember as a mason – but it did have a lot of Bible verses in it alongside the information. At least, as far as I know it did – he wasn't allowed to show the contents to me or even really talk about it, and although I joked with him, I respected his wishes and let him keep it all secret.

I used to pick him up and drop him off at meetings at the Great Eastern Hotel in Liverpool Street. He used to come out of there rolling drunk, but he'd clearly enjoyed himself. He'd meet up with blokes and talk about the war; it was just like a big boys' club really. In the car, I'd joke with him that I'd been reading his little Bible, and he'd get very flustered because it was supposed to be secret and he wasn't meant to show it to anyone. I hadn't really read it, of course, but I used to nick it off him from time to time, for a laugh.

Although he was secretive about what actually went on at his meetings, he was also very open and proud about the fact that he attended. He had a certificate on the wall, and a uniform with a sash that he used to wear. He'd also tell anyone who'd listen about all the good works of the Freemasons; about the hospital that they ran and how they looked after children.

One Saturday night in 1985, he was watching television with my mum, and she went to bed early and left him downstairs. She came back down just after midnight, and he was just sitting in his chair, with his legs crossed, and his glasses down on his nose. He'd had a massive heart attack, and this time it finished him off. He probably just died in his sleep and never knew anything about it. Mum's neighbour phoned me and in a quivering voice said: 'Arthur, your dad's gone.'

'Gone?' I replied. 'Where's he gone now?'

I assumed that he'd gone out with his friends to get drunk, and they needed me to fetch him.

'No, Arthur, I mean he's gone. Your dad's dead.'

I drove straight round there with Jacqui and the kids. He was sitting there, so peaceful that it was hard to feel sad. Yet a different emotion came over me, and it was surprising: I was angry. I couldn't help feeling that the old man had killed himself by choosing to live his life in the way that he did. He ate terribly, his drinking was even worse, and his smoking habit – which doctors later said was what killed him – was excessive and careless. They were all things that he could have changed if he'd wanted to, and in doing so he might have preserved his life by many years.

Like a lot of men in the 1950s and 60s, my dad was always working long hours; away to work before I got up in the morning, and home after I went to bed. That meant that my brothers, sister and I never really got a chance to know him, as a man, until a lot later in life. I'd just been building a great friendship with him, and now he was gone. He was only in his early sixties when he died, and he could have lived a lot longer. I felt cheated, but after my anger died down, I did something that night that I very rarely did: I cried.

Dad's heart attack was the last of many. He'd had one in my car a couple of months earlier, and I'd had to drive him to the hospital and carry him in. After he recovered from that one – his eighth heart attack, I believe – I lectured him about his lifestyle, and told him that unless he wanted to die, he needed to make some changes. He didn't listen though. I think he must have thought that he was invincible. Perhaps that's a family trait.

3

Back in Training

When James got seriously ill, I took the decision to take a break from powerlifting. To do my involvement in the sport any justice, I needed to be training regularly, and with Jacqui at the hospital so much, there was just no time for me to do it. I couldn't compete without training and I didn't have time to train, so I stepped away and wasn't entirely sure that I'd ever go back. In fact, as James recovered and I started to build my construction business and the relationship with my dad, I chose not to go back. There were many other things in my life, and my thirst for sport had been subdued.

The business continued to grow, and I found myself turning over several million pounds a year. I had quite a few men working for me, but I was the owner and the boss, so I was in a great financial position. With that going well and James on the mend, I found that I had more time to devote to training again. My first tournament after the break was the 1985 European Championships. I didn't lift particularly well and got the bronze medal. Then the old man died, and I took another break, not starting serious training again until 1986. By then my business was becoming very successful, meaning I had even more time to devote to my sport, and all my powerlifting associates were calling me to ask when I was going to compete again. This time I took training even more seriously, and did so with slightly higher quantities of drugs. I competed in the British Championships in 1987, fully expecting to win, but only managed second place. I went on from there to pick up a second silver in the 1987 World Championships.

I'd been lucky with drug testing up to that point. It was random, and thankfully for me, fairly rare. And just in case, I had an insurance policy – I took a masking drug called gonatrophin. It came as an injection, through a huge needle, and just one look at it was enough to put you off. But I needed to ensure I wasn't caught so I took it whenever I was competing – through an injection in my backside. At the 1988 European Championships in Germany though, my luck ran out. I took the masking drug, just as before, but this time it didn't do its job. And as it happened, this was the time that I found myself being asked to take a test. I was confident that my test result would put me in the clear, but my confidence was misplaced. Which was especially embarrassing considering I'd just won the European title . . .

I think, even though I'd taken the masking drug, I knew deep down that I was going to get caught. There was a delay between taking the test and finding out the result, so I went back to my hotel with the rest of the British team to get changed for the evening banquet. We were driven through the mountains around Munich, a beautiful place, in a minibus and I'd won and lifted very well. I'd beaten two world champions to win the European title, and I was sitting at the front of the bus with a gold medal strung around my neck. Everyone else on the team was saying, 'You were great, you done good' but I was a bit quiet. I couldn't help replaying the drug test in my mind, over and over again, and wondering if the masking drug was going to save me. I knew there was a chance that I could come unstuck here.

Then, and this is the truth, an enormous clap of thunder came from the mountains, and shook the entire valley. My first thought, which I will always remember, was that the game was up, and this was God telling me so. I reckon that sudden thunderclap, which came from nowhere and disappeared just as fast, was God saying 'You're in trouble now, you're finished.' And if it was, he was right. The food at the banquet stuck in my throat. Six months later, I was officially stripped of my title and medal, and was on my way to a year's ban from the sport's governing body.

A year earlier, I'd decided to downsize the business. Jacqui had looked over the books while we were on holiday and realised that the gap between turnover and profit was far bigger than it should have been – mainly due to the amount I was paying out in wages to the blokes who worked for me. We did a few sums on the beach in Lanzarote, and I worked out that I could make the same profit with a far smaller turnover and staff, if I just took on the right private contracts. So that's what I did when I returned. And while the plan worked fairly well, it did mean that my income decreased slightly. Problem was, I was paying out a fair amount to Jim Duncan for the gear he was supplying me.

Being a man of my size and strength, I was often being approached by blokes in the gym who knew of some door work or nightclub bouncing that was available. I'd always laughed it off before, but the drugs I was using cost a lot of money. So, while I was making the transition between the larger business and the more streamlined version, I decided to take one of them up on the offer. There was a country club, not far from where I lived and worked, which needed someone for the occasional evening shift. The money was pretty good and there were also certain 'perks' which made it more worthwhile.

So, early in 1988, I started working at this country club – occasionally at first, then more regularly. It was strange for me to spend so much time in a nightspot as I'd previously stayed away from this sort of place, apart from when I was abroad with the British powerlifting team. Generally though, I didn't spend too much time in British pubs and clubs up to that point.

Around that time, I knew this stocky little power-lifter called Elton, who was quite a bit younger than me. When he decided to clean up and give up his steroid habit, he became so paranoid that he wouldn't come out of his house. He was a short bloke, a lightweight, and relatively skinny, too. Even on the steroids he only weighed 75 kg, but with their help he maintained an awesome muscular physique. But when he went clean, he became paranoid that he was only half the man he should have been, so he'd lock himself away for days on end, refusing to go outside. In the middle of all this drug culture, two of the biggest factors were bravado and ego, and that meant that none of us would ever admit to being dependent on the gear. You might say it 'just helped you along' but you would always maintain that you didn't need it, and you were always totally in control. But that wasn't really true at all, as I discovered. The drugs controlled you.

Although I'd been using drugs in various forms for around six years, I always took them for what I considered a purpose, to fuel training or give me a boost in competition. But while I'd thought I could live without them, I was kidding myself. It's not clear to me when the transition took place, but by 1988 I'd realised that it had become an addiction, and worse still, a dependency. In the early years of my drug use, I would never go looking for a fix. Someone would ask if I wanted a bit of this or a bit of that – just as if it was a cigarette – and I'd take it. But it was either a casual thing or else just a part of my powerlifting. From that year, especially as my social circle expanded through door work at the country club, I started taking so-called recreational drugs, and cocaine in particular, much more regularly. Even then I still didn't have to go looking for it. It was always there, available, it would find me. I wasn't a religious man, but someone 'down there' was definitely helping me to get deeper and deeper into this. People – some of whom I hardly knew –

would come up to me at the door of the club and shake my hand.

'Hello Arthur, how are ya?'

As we shook, they'd slip me something. Of course, I knew what it was. They weren't slipping me a fiver. They were trying to buy their way into the club, or into my favour. So I never had to go looking, it was always there, and in big quantities, too. Sometimes I'd be handed a bag of the stuff weighing a pound.

I was now simply being handed more coke than I knew what to do with, yet it wasn't always like that. When I was first getting into it, I got it from my friend Jim Duncan, who had been providing me with steroids and speed previously. Unlike many wiser suppliers, Jim was prepared to use the stuff he sold, even though he'd had a quadruple heart bypass due to steroid abuse in the past. Jim and I were very good mates, and although he introduced me to all these things, I don't put the blame on his shoulders for my addictions. Only one person can be held responsible for the drugs I took, and the things I did because of them, and that's me.

After a few months working at the country club, I saw a pal of mine who was a wrestler on a heavy drinking session. He was with a mate of his, a wealthy builder named Mark O'Leary, and Mark had clearly had too much to drink. We had a fairly strict door policy, and I decided that he'd misbehaved enough, and got ready to throw him out. Seeing that I was about to feel his collar, Mark made me an offer in an attempt to pacify me:

'If you ever want a job, come and see me,' he said with a smile, and handed me his card.

The situation calmed down, and Mark and my wrestler friend chose to leave the club anyway. A few days later though, I saw an advert in the paper from a company called O'Leary Construction, Mark's company. They were looking for site agents, and paying about £400–£500 a week. Even though I was still running my business, which I had recently downsized, I gave Mark a call. There was a good reason for that – after downsizing the company to focus on a few large clients, I ended up getting stitched up, and it left me in a less secure financial position. I had a big contract with this one company, where I did the work for cost plus 10 per cent. I did just over a million pounds of work for them, so at the end of the year I was expecting somewhere in the region of £130K. But the company did the dirty on me, and I ended up with about £35K, which, while it was good money, left me severely down on what I was expecting. I realised that I needed to go jobbing, so to speak, and that the future of my business was now unsure.

Mark was my first point of call, and he happily gave me a job as a site agent, running a building site for just under £500 a week. That was good enough money for me, especially combined with increasing amounts of door work, and meant that I could relax a bit – I'd realised that working for yourself could be exhausting, leaving little time for anything else. So I wound up the business and used the £35K I'd made to buy a villa in Spain. I also moved us to a bigger house in Loughton, and we had no mortgage to pay. In 2006, that house sold for just under a million pounds. Sadly, it had long left my possession by that point.

I enjoyed bringing home plenty of money and giving up the business meant that my earning potential had dipped. I was used to some of the 'finer' things – nice holidays, driving a Jag, and of course, plenty of illegal substances. In order to make sure that I didn't lose any of that, I took on further door work around Essex and East London. One of the more notorious venues to recruit me was a club called the Green Gate, in Ilford. Weeknights there were generally quiet, with only the occasional 'incident'. We made the definition between 'incidents' and 'fights', because the odd scuffle between a couple of blokes was nothing, at least in comparison to what would often happen on a Saturday night. A 'fight' was the epitome of the Saturday nightclub scene – there would always be kids out looking for a battle – and me and my pals would get stuck right in the middle.

The club was well known as a place for kids who got fuelled up on drugs and drink and wanted to fight, and so as a doorman you knew that whenever you went to work there on certain nights, you were going to have a fight to handle. During one such fight, one of my fellow doormen got hit with a golf club and it killed him.

Another time, I got myself seriously hurt, too. It was a Saturday, there was a huge fight, and a bloke went for one of my mates with a lead pipe. I got it out of his hand, and started bashing him with it. I should have left it there, but moments like that were always so intense that something would drive you on, and make you keep going. I chased him out of the club, and down the road, but there was a kerb which I hadn't spotted, and I tripped up on it. I fell over and hit my head on the pavement, stunning myself briefly and losing my grip on the weapon. He turned, swiftly gathered a few of his mates, and together they gave me a huge beating – one which I would not have survived had it not been for my protective physique. I curled into a ball as kicks, punches and blows from the weapon rained down on my body. By the time they'd finished, my face had swollen up like a balloon. When Jacqui woke up in the morning and saw my face lying next to her, she screamed.

Fights were regular occurrences at all the clubs where I worked. Although I'd been in a few scraps at school, and built my body up into a powerhouse since then, I hadn't been involved in any real violence in my life. The door work changed all that, as I was plunged headfirst into this violent culture. In a strange way I enjoyed it, even though I knew I wasn't meant to. I always felt that if someone started a fight I'd be able to finish it, and that gave me a warped kind of pride. Just like in those fantasies I would have where I'd walk away from a train wreck, I secretly believed that nothing truly bad could happen to me due to my strength. This is one of the dangers of the steroid abuse: you feel invincible and begin to believe that nothing can touch you.

I didn't think I was a great fighter though. I knew that if I got in the ring with a bare-knuckle fighter like Lenny Mclean, he'd probably knock seven buckets out of me. But on the street it was different; I wasn't frightened of him, or of anyone. I never worried that I could have got myself killed, even though the nature of the work meant creating more and more enemies for myself by the night. Just because I wasn't scared for my life, however, didn't mean I wasn't afraid. There was a certain amount of fear in all of us on the doors, as we wondered what we'd have to get stuck into next. If you're doing a job like that and you say you're not in the least bit frightened, you're lying, but fear produces adrenaline and that moves you forward. It's often fear that creates and fuels the greatest acts of bravery.

Through contacts made on various doors, I also started even more lucrative security work at a load of illegal raves – massive secret parties at which drug abuse wasn't just common, it was practically a requirement of entry. The raves that I ran were called Raindance, and they were run by a guy who still lives in Loughton today. He put me in charge of overseeing the whole thing; we'd have about a hundred and fifty security staff, with fifty or more dogs, to look after twenty thousand kids. There were six of us assigned simply to look after the money. We had yellow baseball caps with Raindance on them; I used to bring them home and give them to the kids.

Working at Raindance had a massive influence on me because it was such a hotbed for drugs. On the door, we'd routinely search a few people for drugs – even though we knew for sure that almost everyone there had come to get high on one thing or another. If we found drugs on a rave-goer, we'd take them away, and as the man in charge, I'd be the one who took them home. Each night, I'd come home with a shoe box full of drugs, and I used to routinely take them, just to see what they were and what they did. We'd give some to the police – to pacify them and demonstrate that we were trying to limit drug abuse – but I'd still come home with over 4 kg worth each time. I had so much that I could afford to take some every single night – which was my introduction to mass drug taking.

4

Donna

I'd been working at the Green Gate for a while and had pretty much become immersed in a violent drug culture. The one part of me that hadn't changed though was my love and commitment for my family, and Jacqui in particular. Let me give you an example: it was midweek, and one of the traditionally younger nights. There was a girl there that night, probably still a teenager, who spotted me on the door and immediately started flirting. At first it was funny – I laughed it off and exchanged a couple of dirty jokes with the guy working the door with me. But she came back, and this time, she was flirting much more heavily. I looked at her as she made me an offer. The answer seemed simple: I was a married man and loved my wife. I didn't want to go down that road. Believe it or not, I was still quite straight in some ways.

To find a hard man who would tell a bunch of blokes that he loved his wife and was faithful was sadly a bit of a rarity. Most of them were looking at the *Sunday Sport* and always trying to 'pull a bird'; that was the norm. When I found myself approached by a woman, as I sometimes did on the door of the Green Gate, I always rejected any advances made towards me.

Until late in 1988, that was . . .

I'd become a regular doorman at the country club, which paid me a decent amount in pocket money and drugs. My job would involve literally standing at the door of the place, and fifteen feet behind me there was a reception counter. Behind that counter was a girl named Donna; she was no more than twenty years old, and very pretty. I acknowledged the fact that she was attractive, like any bloke would, but that was as far as it went. Other doormen tried their luck (even if they were married) and got knocked back, but I wasn't going to allow myself to even think about it. She was a pretty girl, and seemed nice enough, but I didn't need to have too much to do with her, besides saying hello, and helping out if something kicked off at the reception desk.

One night, a young fella turned up at the door.

'I'm Donna's boyfriend,' he told me. 'Can I just go in and see her?'

'Of course you can,' I replied, and stepped aside. She'd told me about him, and I knew they were serious about each other: they may have even been engaged. Punters continued to appear, and I quickly forgot about him. A few minutes later, I heard a row developing behind me. He had started to get very agitated and was swearing at her. I stepped between them and tried to calm the situation down. If this had just been a regular punter, I might have thrown him out right there and then, but this was Donna's boyfriend, and out of respect for her I tried to find a calmer solution.

'Now look mate,' I said, interrupting, 'this isn't on. This is a respectable club, so shut your mouth or get out.' He didn't choose either option. Instead he got even more verbal with Donna, and then with me. Then he started to turn a bit violent, and it was at that point that I lost my patience. I was always prepared to reason with people until it turned physical. Once that line had been crossed, they were always quickly turfed outside. I picked this fella up and simply carried him the fifteen feet to the front door, and ejected him into the night. I walked straight back to Donna, fully expecting an earful of abuse from her. Women are often fiercely loyal to blokes like that, even if they're mistreated by them. Thankfully, Donna wasn't in the least bit unhappy. She told me that they were finished anyway, and was very grateful that I'd got rid of him. She was a streetwise girl, but she was still only young, and didn't need a man being violent around her. It seemed that I had solved a problem for her.

After that, our relationship changed. Where before I'd kept my distance, now we became more friendly. I didn't see why that was a problem – after all, I'd helped her out in a tough spot, and I was just about old enough to be her dad; I was thirty-seven when we met, she was twenty. In fact, Donna seemed to be looking for a father figure. Her parents had got divorced when she was very young and she didn't know all that much about her dad. She certainly didn't know where he was at that time in her life, and she'd taken her mum's maiden name. She'd been brought up by her mum, who was Welsh, and her only close male influence was her brother, who had what would now be termed 'special needs' (at the time, we just said that he wasn't the sharpest knife in the drawer). As I got closer to her, I naturally took on the role of her protector, like an uncle.

Our relationship was still strangely innocent, considering her good looks and my testosterone levels. As I said though, it was a father-figure relationship, based and secured in the fact that we were too far apart in years to worry about any other kind of connection. Donna became even more friendly as the weeks went on; she would come and stand with me at the door, hold my arm and say: 'He's my Uncle Arthur.' But of course, really, I represented everything she wanted in a man. For one thing, I was married, and not just that – I was happily married. She'd met Jacqui at one of our regular staff get-togethers. She saw us there, and we had danced together all night, not sat apart for most of the evening like many other couples. She could see how much we were in love, and afterwards she wouldn't stop talking about how good we were together. I think she craved that kind of happiness.

There were many other things which I had that she wanted. She knew for instance that I had two lovely children and that I was a very successful powerlifter. I had a nice job, a nice car, and a house with no mortgage. Basically, I had everything she wanted for herself, and from a man, and once she realised that, I think she began to feel differently about me. I'm absolutely certain that she didn't fall in love with me – then or ever – but she loved what I represented.

Occasionally, I would give her a lift to her home in Leyton after the club closed at about three or four in the morning. It wasn't a long way out of my way – the round trip was about twenty minutes in total, so it wasn't a problem. I wanted to make sure she got home safely, so, revelling in my role as 'Uncle Arthur', I would take her home, literally just dropping her off. I would never go into her house, even if she invited me in for coffee. I figured that Jacqui probably wouldn't like me doing that, and besides, she lived with her mum.

But then her mum moved back to Wales. Donna had a life in London, and didn't want to leave that behind, so stayed and moved in with one of her friends. It was still roughly on my route home, so I would continue to give her a lift. Before long, I seemed to be doing it every time we were on a shift together. For some reason, now that I was dropping her off at this new flat, she would often lean over before getting out of the car and give me a peck on the cheek to say good night. I didn't really notice this transition at the time; it seemed like a normal enough thing to do.

Very slowly, and very subtly, the nature of our relationship began to change. It was all still pretty innocent, but I was becoming less of an uncle, and more of a friend. When we met each night at the club, for instance, I would say 'hello darling' and give her a kiss. Physically, there was never anything heavier than that, but a line had been crossed between non-contact and contact. Occasionally, she and I would joke about going out with each other –

when I'd asked her jokingly for her phone number, she'd replied that she wouldn't give it to me as I was old enough to be her dad – but then eventually we did meet for a drink before work, although, again, it went no further. I still wasn't looking at her in that way – I thought to myself that even if I did become interested in her, deciding to do the dirty on Jacqui, I knew it would be a waste of time trying to make a pass at a gorgeous-looking girl like that. She was a stunner – a curvy blonde with the sort of figure that made her friends jealous. She'd had lots of boyfriends, and lots of men after her who were much younger than me. She was the life and soul of the party, often off her head on cocaine, and everyone who knew her, liked her. So even if there might have been a small part of me that thought about her in that way, I really didn't think too much about it.

Donna became very seriously ill at the end of 1988. It may have been related to her drug-taking, but whatever it was, it was serious enough to force her to go to Wales to be with her mother. I started far fewer shifts at the country club at the same time as she left because I'd been offered better-paid work at another club called Charlie Chan's (which is now a very serious nightclub).

One night, one of the waitresses there came up to me. I vaguely knew her, or at least knew of her; she was a good friend of Donna's. She put a piece of paper in my hand. I opened it, and saw that it had a phone number written on it.

'I've spoken to Donna,' she said.

'How is she?' I asked, genuinely concerned.

'She's a lot better. She asked me to pass this on to you. It's her phone number in Cardiff.'

I felt a mix of responses. I'd begun to find myself more and more attracted to Donna and it had been an attraction that I'd felt a little guilty about, even though nothing had happened. When she moved out of the picture, I'd breathed a bit of a sigh of relief that I was no longer feeling that kind of extra-marital temptation. At the same time though, I liked Donna an awful lot, and in more than one way – and now she was going out of her way to get in touch with me. I wasn't sure what to do, until I remembered something. I was due to go to Cardiff anyway, a couple of weeks later, to officiate at a powerlifting competition. There could be no harm, I reasoned, in just saying 'hello' when I was down there.

I went down to Cardiff as planned, and decided to stay the night in the Holiday Inn hotel, just outside the city centre. Almost as soon as I got into my room, I picked up the phone and dialled. Donna answered:

'Hello.'

'Donna? It's Arthur,' I said.

'Arthur!' came the reply. 'This is a nice surprise. Where are you?'

'Actually, would you believe it, I'm in your neck of the woods.'

'Really?' The excitement in her voice was infectious and gave me boldness.

'Have you eaten yet?' I asked, characteristically thinking of my stomach. 'Maybe we could meet up for a meal? Could you get a cab over to my hotel?'

I told her to come over at 8 p.m., and booked a table at the hotel restaurant. At 7.30 p.m., I got a call from reception to say that she was waiting there for me. I'd just stepped out of the shower to answer the phone, and was wearing nothing but a towel, so I asked her to wait there for me. Frantically, I set about drying myself and coating my body in aftershave. Suddenly, there was a knock at my door.

'Arthur?' came Donna's voice, half-whispered with nervous excitement.

'I'm not quite ready,' I pleaded.

'It's OK, I'll just wait for you,' she said.

I opened the door, still wearing just a towel, and saw her for the first time in months. Predictably, she was dressed to kill, wearing the kind of little black dress that would have turned any man's head.

'Wow,' I thought, and possibly said.

I got dressed quickly while she sat on my bed. Despite the obvious sexual tension, my stomach was ruling my head as ever.

'Come on then,' I said, standing by the door. 'Let's get something to eat. I'm bleedin' hungry!' The average powerlifter's diet would make most regular people's eyes bulge – I'd eat a whole chicken before going out to lift – and I hadn't eaten at all since lunchtime.

Donna had other ideas. 'Why don't we call room service instead?' she asked.

I didn't think to argue – this way we'd get the food even faster. I called room service and ordered plenty of food and wine.

I wasn't stupid. By now I was thinking that something could happen here, and to be honest, I was hoping. Jacqui was out of sight in London, and out of mind, or at least so I thought. I wasn't entirely certain of Donna's intentions, even though I had a pretty good idea. So I decided to keep on playing innocent, just in case I'd got it wrong, and to make sure that I still got to eat!

The food arrived, as did the wine, which helped us both relax. Before long we were filling each other in on the last few months, and laughing about our time at the country club. The laughter turned to affection, the affection turned into passion. Before long, we were in bed together.

Without wanting to be too explicit, it wasn't a great sexual experience. Although while we were flirting, I didn't really think about Jacqui, once we'd started getting physical, the guilt descended on me like a dark cloud. I just couldn't perform. All I could think about was Jacqui and the kids. As far as it went as an exciting sexual encounter, it was pretty much a damp squib. It was obvious to me that Donna didn't feel satisfied sexually, but on the other hand I knew she wasn't unhappy, and so it wasn't a terrible experience for me either. She felt comfortable in my company, and was clearly pleased to have finally got closer to me. I'm no psychologist, but I think part of it was that father-figure connection again. I called a taxi for Donna in the early hours, and I drove home after the competition the next day.

When I got home, to be met by a smiling Jacqui and our two lovely children, I felt terribly guilty. Yet I was also well aware that I had completely got away with it; she wasn't in the least bit suspicious. I realised then, terrible as this is, that I could pretty much get away with anything. Within a couple of days, I'd spoken to Donna again, and she'd made it clear that she'd like to see me again. And where before I'd have tried to resist temptation, now a line had been crossed and there was no going back.

We started to meet up regularly for sex. I would find any excuse I could to go to Wales and see her. I'd tell Jacqui that I was working a shift at Charlie Chan's, and then shoot off from my day job in Essex a little bit early, around four. There were a lot fewer cars on the road back then, and I could get to Cardiff in about three hours. Once I got there, I'd book into a hotel where Donna would be waiting, spend a few hours with her, and then leave her there, sleeping, at about one in the morning. I'd roll in around four, which of course was totally normal. Jacqui just thought that I'd gone straight from work to the gym, and then straight from the gym to the door job – just as I might normally do.

Jacqui didn't have a clue about what was going on; she was completely in the dark. I was earning good money, and with all the 'gifts' I'd pick up on the door, I could earn in three nights what other blokes earned in four. It was fairly easy then for me to tell her that I was working and take the night off instead.

What surprised me though, was the sex. It was awful. We were supposed to be having this red-hot sexual liaison, and yet it just never seemed to work. It was all my fault; every time we got into bed, that same cloud of deceit descended on me. It wasn't that I was picturing Jacqui or anything like that, I simply knew that this was wrong, and that I was doing something that I really shouldn't have been.

I was getting pretty tired of the motorway journey to and from Wales, so I was pleased when Donna told me that she didn't want to stay there any longer. She wanted to come back to London, where all her friends were. She didn't have much money though, and what she had she usually wasted on nights out, so she relied on me for help. O'Leary's (my day job) had a contract with a painting and decorating shop in Collier Row, and I heard through them that they had a flat upstairs that was available to rent. Because Jacqui had no real idea what I was earning at Chan's, I decided to pay for the flat for Donna out of the door money I was earning. I even helped her to move in and decorate it. I liked having her close by, and also having somewhere to be alone with her without having to pay out for a hotel.

I started to see her even more often; she got a job waitressing at Charlie Chan's. Now I was spending time with her every day, and our relationship seamlessly progressed. No longer was it just a sexual relationship – probably a good thing considering how disastrous that side of things had been – now it was a full-blown affair. People started to get to know about us, just a few at first, but since Jacqui rarely went anywhere near the club scene there was little need to keep it a secret from anyone in that community. Now Donna would regularly come up to see me when I was on the door and act like she was my girl. Blokes stopped chatting her up because they knew she was with me, and she didn't have another relationship because she saw it that way, too.

Donna was still dabbling fairly heavily in drugs, and considering that she didn't have a lot of money, that meant her getting in with some very serious people. At the time, most of the drugs in the South of England were controlled by a gang in Basildon. She would go down quite regularly to see them, to buy a bit of gear, and to pick up a bit more to sell for them. She was a mouthy girl, and sometimes she would come back from there with a black eye; she'd given someone a bit of abuse and they'd whacked her. Once, I went down there to 'sort out' someone who'd hit her. When I got there, however, I realised I was well out of my depth. These were some seriously heavy people. I never dealt directly with these 'friends' of Donna's, just had occasional brushes with them.

'Keep your mouth shut,' I warned her, 'or it's going to get you, and me, into trouble.'

Donna's drug-fuelled mouth caused her no end of problems. She was onto a good thing waitressing at Chan's, but she managed to talk her way out of it by having one too many arguments with her manager. She fell on her feet though, and landed herself a job on the perfume counter of a department store in West London. She earned good money – she knew how to play the part and she was on commission. She was also earning pocket money from selling cocaine for the Basildon gang, so she became slightly less dependent on me. My reaction was to be even more generous – I bought her a Ford Escort convertible, and I talked about saving up to buy her a Porsche.

The affair continued well into 1989, right under Jacqui's nose. She had no idea what was going on. Over that time our relationship had understandably weakened, although she probably wasn't sure why. I was spending so much time away from the house, supposedly at work or the gym, that we rarely spent any quality time together. She looked after the children, and I worked and trained. That was the nature of our marriage at that stage. Thinking purely selfishly, I wasn't getting all that much out of it. Then, I began to think about something which had never even crossed my mind before, and which I never imagined would do: I started to think about leaving Jacqui.

At the same time, those intense feelings of guilt when I was with Donna weren't going away. Our sex life was still terrible – even though our relationship was basically built on lust. For Donna, though, sex wasn't the important thing. What mattered to her was that I was the man that she wanted, and as she saw it, I could give her the kind of love and security that I'd been giving my wife.

But of course, that wasn't exactly true. For a start, I didn't love Donna. I thought she was gorgeous, and I was pretty proud to have a twenty-year-old blonde on my arm, but our relationship was one dimensional. In contrast, Jacqui and I had grown up together and come through good times and bad – from the joy of seeing our children born to the hell of James's illness. When you've had all that with one person over two decades, it's very hard to manufacture it with someone else. And there was so much that Jacqui had that Donna didn't – she could make me laugh, she was much more intelligent, she was the sort of woman you'd want to spend your life with. What's more, my sexual relationship with Jacqui had always been brilliant. What an irony – I was having a sexual affair, but the sex was much better with my wife!

All these thoughts and feelings were swimming around in the back of my mind. In the long-term, I couldn't see the affair going anywhere, and the guilt was crippling it anyway. It was all a bit of a disaster – yet I kept on going. Perhaps it was my pride, or perhaps I enjoyed the excitement of doing something bad, but I kept seeing Donna. Even though I knew it was doomed to failure from the outset, our relationship was just another addiction. And just as I thought that I was in control of my steroid and cocaine addiction, I believed that I knew what I was getting into with Donna, and could stop at any time if I needed to. But just like the drugs, the affair had me in its grasp, and soon it was controlling me.

5

Guns

My life was starting to get darker and darker. I was having an affair, I was addicted to steroids and cocaine, and I'd been banned from my sport for failing a drugs test. Working on the door, I was having more and more violent experiences, ejecting punters who didn't want to leave, or breaking up fights on the dance floor or the street.

I was still doing the Raindance raves, simply because I could earn so much money from a night's work. They were illegal though, and that meant that there were bigger risks involved. I received a tip-off one night that a gang of blokes were planning to come down and rob us. This event raised an awful lot of money – all these kids were paying £20 each to get in so there was over a quarter of a million taken on the door. We would literally stuff all these twenty pound notes into black sacks and store them in a little hut opposite the door. Just as predicted, a team of men did turn up, looking to rob us. They'd underestimated us, though, and hadn't realised how many security staff we had. A group of us faced them down at the gate and administered a beating. Some of them had weapons, but they were no match for our numbers. I wasn't into knives and guns – the biggest thing I had with me was a pick-axe handle. Besides, they were just a bunch of kids who thought they were being opportunists.

Working down at Chan's, however, we got involved with a different kind of clientele. The men who went in there were real gangsters and crooks, serious men. If I searched a bloke like that and found a gun, I'd just let him take it in there because I knew someone like that would shoot me before he'd let me take his weapon. I didn't much like guns myself – believing myself to be invincible of course, I had no need for them – and the most serious knife I owned was the one I used to chop steak. Although I was involved in a few shady things, generally I was well liked and respected. I didn't have many enemies around, and I didn't have any beef with particularly violent or serious men.

Donna was getting further involved with the Basildon mob, though, and she was still letting her mouth get her into trouble. Several more times, I'd have to go down there to meet blokes and talk to them to try to get her out of difficulty, and that meant that my face was getting known. For the first time, I started thinking about arming myself – just for when I went down there. It probably wasn't safe, I reasoned, to go down there without a weapon.

One of the people I knew from working at the country club was a guy called Billy Dando. We trained together, too, and I got to know that his passion outside lifting was the military. He wasn't a soldier, but he was really into anything to do with the army, especially guns. Occasionally, he would come in to the club 'tooled up', that is, with a gun concealed on him. There were a few others who would come into the club armed, but Billy was the one who was really into them. He loved the things, and talked about them all the time.

It's hard to forget my first close-range encounter with a gun. Billy picked me up one night for work in his horrible old orange Morris Marina, and I had to move a little string bag off the passenger seat when I got in. He said there was a bloke coming down to pick it up, and that we should keep it on the door ready to give to him. If he was inside, sorting out some trouble, I should keep an eye out for this man and hand it all over to him.

'What's in it?' I asked.

'It's just a little .38 Beretta,' he replied casually. 'With maybe twenty or thirty shells. It's broken.'

I tried not to sound surprised. As I've said, I wasn't the biggest fan of guns, so I regarded the bag with a little suspicion.

'What's wrong with it?'

'It's jammed. He should be able to sort it out.'

At Billy's request, I took the gun and the shells out of the bag and put them in my pocket. It was a tiny little thing, no bigger than a modern mobile phone, and it seemed ridiculous to think that something so small could cause so much damage. It's unlikely you'd use it at any great distance, but at close range you could use this little thing to kill someone.

It was a regular night on the door, and for the most part, quite slow. All evening I had the gun in my pocket – loaded but jammed – and so as time dragged on, I began to play with it. I was just fidgeting, clicking this useless trigger again and again – click, click, click.

The night went on. I was standing on the door with another bloke, clicking this little Beretta in my pocket, when I realised that I hadn't seen Billy for some time. Then almost straight away, we heard that there was some aggravation inside, so the two of us headed that way. Billy was on the edge of the bar, talking to these two guys who'd had a bit of an argument. It seemed to have calmed down, so I nodded to my fellow doorman to stand down and hang in the background. There was still a fair amount of tension though, so I kept clicking the Beretta even more. Click, click, click.

One of the men started getting more agitated again, and a few of his friends began to gather near-by. I could see that within seconds we were going to have a situation on our hands, and I began to pre-pare myself for a ruck, still clicking furiously. Click, click, click. Click, click, click . . .

BANG!

There were a few screams, and a fair few people hit the floor. I didn't realise at first, but somehow, the gun had gone off in my pocket. How I didn't shoot myself in the foot I'll never know – the bullet had gone through my trousers and hit the angry bloke in the knee. The bullet whipped his leg from beneath him, and as he tried to react, he ended up doing a kind of somersault in mid-air before coming crashing to the ground. In a strange way, it was almost funny. It wasn't a serious injury, but then quite often with gunshot wounds it is the shock that kills you, not the bullet.

As this guy hit the ground, everything stopped instantly. The DJ pulled the music; people scattered, emptying the club. Billy and I just grabbed this injured fella, and threw him out. None of his friends were going to put up any resistance after that – even though it had been a complete accident.

I told the rest of the door staff how it had happened by accident, and at the time they laughed. Yet before long, it had gone around most of our local fraternity that Arthur White was carrying a gun. For people, it figured – it was just the next stage that I had predictably hit, carrying a gun. It wasn't true though.

A few weeks later, I had another run in with firearms, and this time it was enough to convince me to start talking to Billy about arming myself. A few of us, including Billy, were standing on the door of the country club one night when a Transit van came racing around the corner and slowed down right in front of the club. Someone inside emptied both barrels of a twelve-bore shotgun, right in our direction, but fortunately the shooter didn't appear to be accurate. The shots whistled right over the top of my head; had I been a taller man, they might have entered my brain. You can still see today the pit marks where the shot hit the wall, thankfully without causing harm. The van pulled away, leaving us shaken, and we assumed that they had meant to warn, rather than hit us.

Charlie Chan's was a far more serious nightclub, and that meant that occasionally it was a very dangerous place to work as a doorman. The club was in Walthamstow, in the East End of London, and was part of the famous Walthamstow greyhound track stadium. It was owned by the same people as the dog track, and it was a very, very popular club. It was an adult club, meaning that you never got teenagers in there. We had a strict door code; you wouldn't get in if you were under twenty-one, and on many nights we'd raise the age bar to twenty-five.

The older clientele meant that you had men and women who weren't afraid to spend serious money on a night out, and that meant that you'd often see many of the East End's most infamous characters in there. Now I was there, too, and rubbing shoulders with these people. I became fairly well known, and well liked. I was a champion powerlifter, which always opened up doors and gained me plenty of respect. In fact, despite my ban, at that time I was a world champion.

After I was banned by the British Weightlifting Association, it meant that I couldn't compete in the premier powerlifting world championship. But there was a second championship – not quite as prestigious at that time, but still well known and regarded – and the organising body (called the World Powerlifting Congress or WPC) were prepared to overlook my ban and drug test results, and allow me to compete in their competitions. I flew to Johannesburg, South Africa, late in 1988, for their World Championship. That in itself was a big decision – by flying to South Africa and competing there, I knew I'd get a lifetime ban from the British Weightlifting Association. At that time, the Gleneagles convention had barred international sportsmen from competing in South Africa during apartheid, and a breach of the convention meant an automatic lifetime ban, which indeed I got. I didn't care though – I wasn't about to sit around waiting for a whole year, wasting time, serving that ban. I'd made my choice to step across to the WPC and I was happy with it.

All sporting bodies need to be recognised by the IOC in order to be officially considered 'sporting'. If not, competition isn't illegal, but it's not recognised as a sport. The WPC, being a fledgling organisation, didn't yet fit into the 'official' category, but then I didn't much care about official recognition. What really mattered to me was that the WPC didn't bother with drugs testing, and that meant that I could hit the gear and cocaine as hard as I liked.

The day of the competition arrived. I was thirty-eight, and I was going to be competing against the biggest star of the WPC, a great bear of a man called Thor Kristy, who was fourteen years my junior. This was my debut in the WPC, and I was a bit of an unknown factor, despite my successes in Britain and Europe. Since I knew they didn't drug test, I was bang on the gear when I got up to lift. It wasn't easy, but powered by the steroids, I managed to beat Kristy and win the competition – which came as a complete shock to my opponent. It was my first world title, and I was a very proud man. It didn't even enter my head that I had only won because of the drugs – all that mattered to me was that I'd won, and could call myself a world champion.

Most people weren't too aware of the intricacies of powerlifting, so they just knew that I was a world champion, and that was good enough for them. People – those kinds of people – liked to be able to say that they knew a world champion athlete, especially in a strongman's sport like powerlifting. So then, as I was well known for this and the feat of strengths I'd performed to win such a title, I obviously didn't have to do anything to prove a reputation. If I was a world champion (and then subsequently British champion, competing under the British Powerlifting Organ-isation), I was clearly a lot stronger than most of them. That was initially what got me door work, of course, and keeping up that image was what kept me in plenty more work. And if I ever did get into any trouble on the door, it was my strength that got me out of bother, rather than an ability to fight. I was never a particularly great fighter, but if I got hold of someone, he would have trouble getting away from me.

Once I became involved in the more lively, grown-up club scene, trouble was never far away. There were rivalries between clubs, and even between the doormen who worked at these rival clubs, and sometimes it spilled over into violence. Once, it got really serious.

There was a bit of trouble between our doormen and the blokes who worked at this other club nearby. A few of our guys had ended up in a fight with a few of theirs, and ours had come off worse. Billy, who'd been involved in the fracas, was determined that 'we'd' get revenge on 'them'. He told me that after we closed that night, a few of our boys were going around to this other place to sort these doormen out. He asked me if I wanted to go, and for the first time in my adult life, I agreed to get involved in someone else's fight. It was the sort of thing I used to do at school – wading into a fight to help out a friend – but not something I went looking for now. I was changing: day by day, step by step, I was becoming further and further involved in this violent culture. I was becoming a violent man.

The shift finished, and I joined the rest of the door staff in the car park around the back of the club. Suddenly I, like the rest of the group, was handed a gun. And not just any gun – an automatic machine gun, capable of firing eight rounds a second. I started to have second thoughts – in fact my immediate reaction was simply 'Oops!' I knew then that I should probably have turned Billy down, but I was committed, and now I had to see it through. The ringleader maintained that these were to be taken along 'just in case', but that didn't reassure me. I was holding a gun that could earn me seven years in prison if I got caught with it. Billy and I immediately exchanged words, and agreed that if it got silly, we'd be off. But it was about to get ridiculous.

We were still standing there in the car park, and I was starting to wonder why we hadn't yet moved, when the answer rumbled into view. This P100 pick-up truck pulled up, with a tarpaulin pulled over something on the back. The driver got out, and pulled the tarpaulin down. Underneath was a Bren gun on a tripod; a really serious piece of kit. This thing was a killing machine – it would literally cut your house in half, ripping through brick walls. Minutes later, driving across in a short convoy behind this P100, I couldn't help chuckling to myself. This was madness. It was surreal.

We pulled up outside this club, which by now was silent and empty. It was half past three in the morning, and the whole area was completely silent. That didn't last long though, as we all piled out of our cars. The tarpaulin was pulled back, and the driver of the P100 started to fire the Bren gun at the club. However, the thing about these guns is their sheer power – they spew out round after round, and they're an awesome piece of engineering. They are designed to be bolted down to a secure surface – like the back of the pick-up – but no one had thought to do that: it was just resting in the back of the truck. As three men tried to control this gun and hold it down, a hail of bullets flew out into the night, almost in every direction. It was a miracle that none of us got hurt – let alone anyone else. Bullet after bullet hit every building and fixture around the front of the club – but as far as I could see, not one shot actually hit its target. When the firing finally finished, the club itself appeared to be completely unscathed. There were plenty of holes in other walls, cars, post and telephone boxes, but somehow we'd missed the club! Again, miraculously, we managed not to hurt anyone, although we weren't going to stay around to make sure.

I looked at Billy, and he looked straight back at me with the same expression of sheer shock. 'Let's go,' he said quietly.

We tossed our machine guns into the back of the P100 and left in Billy's car. And after a few minutes driving, we were laughing about it. I was slowly becoming anaesthetised to even the most shocking incidents because the culture of the East End club scene was a culture of madness. Had we turned up two hours earlier, that club could have easily been full, and we could have committed mass murder. Or if these other blokes had been there, after hours, they would have been tooled up, and we could have had a shoot-out in the street – that was the potential of it. It could have been an absolute catastrophe.

6

South Africa

Even though the affair I was having with Donna was riddled with problems – it was all about the sex, yet the sex wasn't working – I continued to plough my time and money into it. Donna and I, in our joint state of denial, even started talking about how I would leave Jacqui. Donna knew that I had two kids, and we both realised that actually leaving them would be a massive wrench for me. To a point, I think Donna was reasonably happy with her life at that time, including our relationship, but she wanted more of me; she wasn't prepared to just go on forever only seeing me in stolen moments. So once every couple of weeks, she'd gently raise the question again.

Throughout I had never been happy with all the deceit and running around behind people's backs. Some blokes and women do it for years, but I didn't like it and all the deceitfulness was really starting to get to me. So as I saw it, I had a choice. Either I could leave Donna behind, and go back to the faithful way of living that had seen me right for the past twenty years, or else I could throw all that away, and commit myself to Donna. The dilemma went around in my head for weeks. If I dropped Donna now, I thought, I'd still probably get away with the whole thing, and Jacqui would never be any the wiser. But then the more red-blooded, lustful side of my character argued back – how could I possibly let go of this young blonde stunner?

In the end, I made up my mind, and immediately decided to act. Because I don't do things by halves, I made a crazy suggestion to Donna.

'Let's just go,' I said.

'Go?' she replied. 'Go where?'

'I want us to be together, but it's got to be away from here. Another country – away from Jacqui and the kids.'

'Where, Arthur?' She looked at me impatiently, as if she thought I was bluffing.

'South Africa.'

At first she was shocked. She'd barely ever been out of the British mainland, and here was I suggesting that we ran away to a country on the other side of the planet. When she realised I was serious, however, she began to think about it. To a girl like her, with few ties and even fewer inhibitions, it sounded exciting. And for me, it seemed far enough away that I might hope to be able to outrun my guilt there.

I hadn't picked that country out of the air though. For a start, I'd been to Johannesburg two years earlier when I lifted in the WPC competition. Added to that, I had a very good friend out there who I knew could sort me out.

Ron Collins was one of my very best pals in powerlifting. Ron, who is now in his seventies, was probably the best powerlifter that England has ever produced. He was seven times World Champion, twelve times European Champion and something like eighteen times British Champion. In the early years of my career, I tried to learn whatever I could from this giant of the sport, and he was quite happy to pass on his experiences to the younger lifters. We became good friends and always kept in touch.

In 1982, Ron had a very shaky year – he got made redundant from his job in the North of England, and he also went through a divorce. He was looking for a new start, so he made a plan to move down to London with his new girlfriend. They'd both sold their houses and were looking for a new property to buy together down south.

Before they could find somewhere suitable, however, Ron got talking to another lifter who lived in South Africa who gave him the idea of going to live out there himself. He decided he would, and immediately started trying to persuade me to follow suit. He would bore me half to death with stories of how cheap the place was – and how much property I could get for my money. I quite liked the idea, too, and even went as far as applying for (and getting) a job out there as a building site agent. At the time, however, James was still ill so Jacqui decided that she didn't feel it was the right thing. I was disappointed, but considering what my wife had been through over the past couple of years, I couldn't really argue. Anyway, Ron went out there and he settled down very happily.

Over the years, I continued to keep in touch with Ron, and kept the dream of moving to South Africa on hold for a later date. I had hoped that perhaps, when the children were older, Jacqui might change her mind. So when Donna and I finally decided that it was time for me to leave Jacqui, the dream re-entered my head. I knew that if we were going to have any chance of working as a couple, we had to get as far away from my family as possible. Being five thousand miles away, South Africa was pretty much exactly that.

I spoke to Ron on the phone and told him what I'd decided. He was shocked, because he'd only ever known Jacqui, and he got on with her well. I don't think he had ever imagined that we'd be going our separate ways, but he was a good mate, so he didn't interfere. I had come to my decision, and as far as he was concerned, I must have had my reasons. He told me that Donna and I were welcome to stay with him for a few days while we sorted out something more permanent.

There was probably a part of me that was frustrated by the fact that I wanted to see a bit more of the world, but had never been able to do so. There was a time in 1980, for instance, when I was offered a job in America but Jacqui didn't want to go. Then in the mid-80s, when we owned a villa in Spain, I wanted us to move the whole family out there, but again, Jacqui didn't want to go. While it wasn't the defining factor, it definitely contributed to my decision to take off. It gave the whole experience a twisted sense of adventure.

I applied for visas for Donna and I to be able to move to South Africa. Foolishly, I left the applications in my briefcase at home. This wasn't because I thought I was untouchable or invincible – it was just me being stupid! Quite legitimately, Jacqui went into my briefcase one day to get our chequebook, and found these two applications. One was labelled 'Arthur White', the other, 'Donna Malone' – a name she'd never previously heard.

She was more confused than shocked. She simply couldn't process the fact that, out of the blue, I'd applied to live in a far off country with a woman she'd never even heard of. Suddenly the air was full of questions – but generally they only had one theme – 'What on earth is going on?'

Now, I've always had a smart mouth and a quick brain, but even I was amazed that I managed to talk my way out of this. We had a row, and I decided that the best course of action was to get angry and play a straight defence. I smashed a cup on the floor, pretending that I was offended by Jacqui's accusations, and I told her that it was none of her business and nothing for her to worry about. Even as I said all this, and as somehow she accepted it, I knew my argument was paper thin. I knew it wouldn't be long before Jacqui worked out what was going on. In fact, this spurred me on to act even more quickly.

I think sometimes, a wife still in love with a cheating husband (or vice versa) will believe any excuse, however weak, because it's better than having to face the truth. Even if that truth is staring them in the face, as it was here, it's somehow easier for them to cope by continuing to swallow the lies of the cheat. That's the only reason I can imagine behind Jacqui's inability to see past my pathetic attempt at a cover story. She'd caught me red-handed, but she was still so much in love with me that she didn't want to believe it.

It wasn't long, however, before Jacqui could deny the truth no longer. A few days later, in November 1989, Donna and I took off for South Africa. I'd had a safety deposit box locked away with my local bank, and I took it out and brought it home when I knew Jacqui was going to be out. There was £35,000 inside, and I took almost all of it with me. I left just £500 in an envelope for Jacqui, marked with little more than 'Goodbye.' I was on a plane with Donna within hours.

I can only imagine what it must have been like for Jacqui to return home from a day out with the kids to find the briefest of 'Dear John' letters and this paltry amount of supposed maintenance money. As I sat on the plane, where I had always imagined I would feel some great sense of relief, I was mired in guilt more than ever. I said very little to Donna, and put away as many drinks as I could get my hands on in an attempt to numb the memory of what I'd done.

South Africa was everything I'd dreamed it would be. Beautiful beaches, clear blue waters, and more cocaine than the hardest addict could ever want. By day we would swim in the ocean, and sun ourselves on sweeping sands; by night we would party hard, spending money like water. I couldn't have been further from the life I'd once known, and, just as I'd hoped, my feelings of guilt began to fade – for a while at least.

As planned, we stayed with Ron for a couple of nights. Ron knew a woman called Sandra who lived nearby, and who originated from Chingford, Essex, not far from where I'd lived in England. She was fairly laid back, but I think secretly it bothered her that I'd run away from my wife and children to be out there with this mistress. She and Donna didn't exactly hit it off, possibly as a result of Sandra's unease. She was much more comfortable with me, however, and we became quite friendly.

One night, I was sitting talking to Sandra, and I thought that Donna had gone to bed. In fact, she was sitting in the next room, and Sandra's walls were not the thickest. Sandra started asking me questions about my family, and since I'd had a drink, I spoke quite openly about the kids, Jacqui, and the life I'd left behind. I didn't say anything particularly earth-shattering, certainly nothing that indicated regret, but suddenly, we heard the front door slam. Donna had been listening, and it had upset her enough to make her want to get out of there.

While, as I said, I didn't tell Sandra that I regretted leaving, communication is about more than simply the words we use. Donna could hear in my voice – even through a wall – that I was missing my wife. She was right of course, the feelings of guilt had now been replaced by something far more significant. I probably wouldn't have told Donna how I was feeling, but she heard it. I ran out of the house after her, and caught up with her in the street. Tears were streaming down her face.

'You're still in love with Jacqui!' she bellowed. 'You're wishing you'd never left her! We've come halfway around the world and all you can think of is her!'

I tried to pacify her. 'No! You've got it wrong Donna. I don't love her.'

To be honest, I wasn't sure who I loved, and what I felt any more. I knew right then that running away like a coward hadn't solved all my problems; it'd just confused them. Unless I faced Jacqui and the kids, and properly ended our marriage, I knew that Donna and I could never have a real life together without being haunted by guilt and 'what ifs'. Right there, in the street, I told her that at some point, I was going to have to go back to England to settle things up, and even though she knew that it might mean that she lost me, Donna agreed.

Donna was unhappy at Sandra's, especially after that, so she persuaded me to buy a property out there. She fell in love with a beach-side flat, two floors up and with a balcony overlooking the sea. Property was generally very cheap to an English buyer, but the £16,000 which I paid to acquire it completely wiped out my savings. The rest had been spent on drink, coke and partying. Once we'd furnished the flat, I had nothing left. That was OK, I rationalised, because I was about to start work as a site agent, and would be bringing in good money. Yet as I handed over the last bit of cash – for a blue striped sofa – I got this desperate, sinking feeling.

Suddenly, I didn't want to come back to England to finish things with Jacqui; I wanted to come home to patch things up with her. I wanted my family back. I realised that I'd been a complete idiot, blowing all our savings on a stupid dream that had now turned sour. Looking at suntanned Donna – if anything she was even more beautiful now – I realised that she and the affair had lost their attraction for me. All these feelings began to rush through my body, and the main theme that this was all wrong. I was going through hell in paradise. Almost as soon as we'd moved into the flat, I announced that I needed to go home to 'sort things out with Jacqui'.

'It's over, isn't it?' Donna asked, holding back the tears. 'You're leaving me and going back to her.'

'No!' I protested, 'I just need to talk to her.' Deep down though, I knew that Donna was right.

That night, two weeks before Christmas, I called Jacqui to tell her that I was coming home, and, faithful as ever, she came to meet me at the airport. Barely a month after I'd left with a holdall full of cash, I returned, penniless. I walked through the arrivals terminal wearing just a T-shirt, jeans and trainers. I didn't even have any bags with me save for one, a holdall filled with my cocaine stash, which arrogantly I'd just carried on to the plane as hand luggage. My usually well-groomed appearance was in tatters. Jacqui said that she didn't recognise me – that I looked like a vagrant. When I reached her, my spirits lifted. I knew I had no right to expect it, but when she flung her arms around me, it felt like the world was being put right again. I handed her the holdall:

'Get rid of that, Jacq. That's been the cause of all my problems.'

In truth though, that was a convenient excuse. I had put a lot of coke up my nose over those last few weeks, but I was always still in control – or at least, that was what I believed. I'd made the conscious decision to leave Jacqui – now I was making a conscious decision to return.

When I finally staggered through the front door of our house in Loughton, I nearly collapsed. I was completely physically and emotionally drained, especially from the increased drug use. When I reached my bed, I slept for what seemed like days.

Christmas was understandably difficult. The overwhelming relief that Jacqui had felt on my return was slowly replaced by anger, unease and mistrust. She was deeply hurt by my 'Dear John' letter, and the manner of my disappearance. When I left for South Africa, I'd told no one that I was going, meaning that she'd had no trail to follow when she'd asked around. She tried desperately to be understanding, and to make a fresh start, but the hurt was still too raw. Those weeks then were a mix of happy times and angry rows. And as the rows worsened, my mind drifted to an unacceptable place.

I began to wonder how Donna was getting on in South Africa. I hadn't been in touch with her for a while, and I imagined that her patience would soon run out. In fact, it already had. I called Donna's mum in Wales to see if she'd heard anything, but I was informed that her daughter had already returned home and was staying with her. Donna had realised that the relationship was over the moment I'd left.

For some reason, this information was to me like a red rag to a bull. Now Donna – this stunning young blonde who couldn't get enough of me – was back in Britain. She was just a three-hour drive away. Almost instantly, the memories of how and why our affair failed seemed to melt away. I had to see her again.

I called Donna to reassure her that our relationship wasn't over after all. She gave me all the right signals, and having just made up my mind to stay faithful to and try harder with my wife and children, I swiftly changed it. I left Jacqui again on New Year's Eve, 1989, just days after promising that I'd never do so again.

Leaving Jacqui and the kids for a second time was heart-wrenching, yet I had managed to convince myself that this was what I truly wanted. I walked to the train station, carrying just a holdall full of clothes, and Jacqui drove alongside me, crying her eyes out, begging me to reconsider. The children were with her, and they, too, were pleading with their dad not to leave again. I just fixed my eyes straight ahead and kept on walking. Inside, my heart was being torn apart by all the emotion I was feeling, yet somehow I managed to keep a lid on it. I finally reached the train station, and as I disappeared inside, I could hear the sobbing of Jacqui and our children behind me. It is a sound that I will probably never forget.

This time, the affair lasted a little longer. Donna and I rented a flat in a village called Sawbridgeworth, in Hertfordshire. It was out in the countryside and gave us a different kind of experience together. Yet before too long – after just a few short weeks – Donna and I remembered exactly why it hadn't worked out for us in South Africa. We were attracted to one another, but when it came down to it, we didn't really have that much in common. We were of different generations and had different interests. Truth be told, we barely even liked each other. It wasn't long before I returned to Jacqui again with my tail between my legs. Not only did she agree to take me back for a second time; she even helped me to clear out the flat that I'd rented with Donna. And while once again she managed to find it in her heart to forgive me, I could tell that I had taken her to an even deeper level of hurt than I had the first time.

Within the space of a few months, I had left my wife, and my mistress, twice each. Somehow, remarkably, both of them still seemed to want me. Jacqui still loved me deeply, although of course she didn't trust me any more. And she was absolutely right not to. Within a few months, I'd left her yet again.

7

Debt Collector

When I went to South Africa, it wasn't just Jacqui who I left hanging. Because we left without telling anyone where we were going – or even in fact that we were leaving at all – I also burned my bridges with every one of my employers. I'd long since sold my business, and the profits had now either been snorted, eaten or tied up in a South African apartment. The company that I had worked for, O'Leary's, were none too impressed by my disappearing act. And my good reputation at the various doors where I'd worked was now seriously tarnished as they realised that I was not quite as responsible as they had previously been led to believe. So not only was I penniless, I also had no job, and no business of my own. I needed to find work, and quickly.

I was talking to my brother Bob over Christmas, and told him that I needed to sort out a quick source of income. He suggested that I got in touch with a friend of his, Paul Grainger, who was owed a bit of money. Perhaps, he said, considering my size and strength, I could offer to do a little bit of debt collecting for him. I'd never made the step into debt collection – clearly we're not talking about the legal kind here – but I knew it was one that many lifters and doormen had eventually made. Obviously there's a lot of money to be made as hired muscle, and while it meant stepping from a legal line of work to an illegal one, the urgency of my finances made the step seem like a small one.

Paul had a fruit and vegetable business at Spitalfields Market, Bishopsgate, East London. Bob took me down there to meet him in a market pub called The Gun, which had a special licence that allowed it to stay open all night for the blokes who worked in the market. Wholesale markets like Spitalfields open in the early hours so that greengrocers and stall holders from across the city can come in during the very small hours, buy their stock for the day, and get back to their shop or stall in time to open.

We walked into The Gun at around 2 a.m., to find Paul, drunk as usual. Paul had a big drink problem, and whenever you met him, you'd always meet him for a drink. We were introduced, and over a game of pool he told me, in slurred speech, that he was owed something in the region of £250,000. That's a lot of money to anyone, but especially in the fruit and veg business, considering that most of the blokes involved are only market traders.

'D'you fink you can get it?' he asked me, impressed by my build.

'Of course,' I said, invincibly as ever.

'So whaddya want?'

I held my nerve. I could have gone in lower, but I looked him straight in the eye. He, of course, was unable to do likewise. 'Seven and a half per cent.' Which was just under twenty grand, and not a bad bit of money.

'Alright,' he slurred, almost without thinking.

And then I really tried my luck. 'I'll want a quarter of it up front, of course.'

I must have caught him on either a very good night, or a very drunk night. Either way, he nodded to one of his entourage, and I got what I had asked for. I sat and finished my game of pool with £5,000 in my pocket – not bad payment for a conversation. I'd not done a stroke, and Paul had no idea that I wasn't even a real debt collector. Of course, putting an envelope full of Paul's money in my jacket meant two things. First, I was going to have to get a result if I didn't want to make myself a very powerful enemy, and second, now, I was a real debt collector.

As it turned out, I didn't have long to wait before I got a chance to prove myself to Paul. We were just finishing our drinks in The Gun when this big geezer walked in. He was another wholesaler, and he had a problem with Paul. He walked straight up to him and started to shout and rave. Well, Paul wasn't a big man – truth be told he'd lose a fight with a paper bag – and this fella chinned him. Paul went crashing to the floor of the pub, and Bob stepped in to intervene. I realised in a flash that this was a perfect opportunity to prove myself to Paul. I pushed my brother aside, and launched myself at this fella. I went at him with everything but the kitchen sink – he never knew what hit him. I hit him a few times, I really bashed him, and the fight was already won. But something came over me: I needed to teach this guy a real lesson, and show off what I could do. On the table, there was an empty bottle of champagne that Paul had drunk his way through, and in a flash of rage, I smashed it into his face. He screamed with pain, absolutely shocked at what I'd done. Then I dragged him outside, weeping, and chucked him into the back of his car. He just lay there, whimpering and bleeding into the seats of his Mercedes.

Paul was very impressed. He asked me to stick around until he'd opened up for the morning, so I joined him at his stand. I soon realised why he'd told me to stay. Within minutes of the market opening, it had gone round the whole market that Paul had got himself a minder, and that his enemies had better beware. All I had to do was stand beside him as he opened up. He had a fat lip, he was seriously drunk, and he was now telling every one of his customers – and many of the other characters from around the market – the story of how I'd bashed this other bloke up. 'You'd better watch yourself,' he told them, before looking proudly across at me, 'I've got protection now.'

Paul was an importer. His business brought fruit and veg into London from the UK and abroad, and he'd sell it on to the other wholesalers, who then sold to grocers and market traders. To my amazement as a fairly experienced businessman, the whole business was run on a system of credit, and this was how Paul frequently ended up with bad debtors.

For instance, a trader might come to Paul and agree a price for some boxes of cucumbers. Paul would write him out a ticket, stating that he could buy the cucumbers at the agreed price, and then the trader would bring that ticket to the cash desk on our stand and pay for the stock. If he didn't have all the money, Paul would very often offer credit, saying 'Pay me for what you bought yesterday and you can pay me for today's when you've got the money.' There was an awful lot of credit, and Paul had a lot of customers, hundreds in fact. And while one bloke might owe twenty quid, another might owe twenty grand. I was amazed that he managed to earn a living this way.

I wasn't surprised to find out that this system was costing Paul a lot of money where debts had gone bad, and he now knew that he had to get a grip on things. That's why he employed me.

Paul wasn't the biggest trader in the market but he was very successful. He made his money by operating a high-turnover, lower profit margin business model. That meant that he upset a lot of people by selling his stuff cheap, sometimes for less than cost in order to drum up more trade. He made a lot of money from operating in this way, and he made sure that everyone knew it, too. A lot of people were therefore very jealous of him, and this gave him plenty of enemies to worry about. In a sense then, he wasn't the safest bloke in the world to be working for in my kind of role.

I started working for Paul, and quickly recouped some of the smaller debts from blokes who took one

look at me and decided that I was not the kind of
fella they'd want to take on. Paul didn't just use me
as a debt collector though, he also used me as a
credit controller – which meant blocking some of
the more dubious transactions. Paul was a bit soft,
and agreed to give someone credit when really he
should have known better. It didn't matter though –
when they reached me on the cash desk, I told them
that their credit was blocked.

I upset a few of the other wholesalers then, and
because stories had spread – many of them exag-
gerated – about how I'd bashed this fella up in The
Gun, word also went around that I was a bit of a
thug and would beat someone up for the heck of it.
This legend about me grew – fuelled by the news
that I was a world champion powerlifter – and my
name was put around as one to be very careful of.

I hadn't carried a weapon since the night Billy
Dando and I had watched a Bren gun making
mincemeat out of masonry. Now, however, I was
concerned that my legend would precede me, and
that therefore the people I went to visit on Paul's
behalf would make sure that they were well prepared for me. I didn't fancy walking up to a bloke
unarmed to find that he was tooled up with a knife
or worse, and so I decided to buy something for my
own protection. I bought a long-bladed diver's

knife, and wore it strapped to my arm, with the handle sticking down so that I could get at it in a hurry.

One of Paul's bigger debtors was an Asian fella known as Black Jack. No one knew his real name but, as he liked a flutter, people knew him by this gambling nickname. He had a very big shop in Green Street, which is near Upton Park, the West Ham United football ground, where there is a large Asian population. A lot of silk trading goes on there – it's sometimes called the Sari centre of Europe. Along there were a number of fruit and veg stalls, and we had accounts with all of them – and not small ones. Jack had one of the biggest, but because he had a bad gambling habit, he'd come out of his shop on a Saturday night with ten or fifteen grand to gamble at the casino, and he'd lose the lot. So, come Monday night when he had to pay us, he never had any money. So I started to go down and collect from Jack, and because of the amounts he owed, I often earned a lot by collecting from him.

I went down there one night, wearing this beautiful silver grey mohair suit, looking very flash. Jack had managed to evade payment for a while, and had racked up a huge amount of credit with Paul. Although in the past he'd been fairly compliant, I had a feeling that this time it was going to be more difficult, and so I took the precaution of wearing my new knife, strapped to my arm.

I went straight through the shop without talking to anyone, and, knowing exactly where the office was, went directly to it. Jack was in there, and I took him by surprise, walking into the office without even knocking on the door.

'What do you think you're playing at, Jack?' I asked, calmly at first.

Jack gave me a load of excuses, but I knew that they were all lies. He'd gambled his money away again – just as he always did.

'I want some money now!' I bellowed, in a voice loud enough to be heard throughout the shop (and the street, for that matter).

Suddenly, I heard the sound of the door closing behind me, and then two little clicks. Instinctively, I knew that they were flick knives. Two of Jack's boys had come in to sort me out, but they clearly had no idea that I was armed. Quoting a line from *Crocodile Dundee*, I pulled the diver's knife out of my sleeve, stuck it in the table, and said: 'This is a knife. Now tell the boys to go away.'

Jack said something to them in his own language and out they went. I'd never intended to use the knife, although undoubtedly I would have done if it had come to it. Thankfully, it did its job, both as a deterrent and a trigger for Jack to miraculously find the money that he owed. He handed me a wad of cash, and I pulled the knife out of the table, and put it back in its sheaf.

The two boys were there, as I walked out – they can't have been more than teenagers – and I just gave them a strong stare as I passed them. They must have hated me, but they knew better than to try it on when I was armed. A very serious incident had been avoided, however. With me being white, if I'd ended up stabbing one of them there could have been a lot of repercussions.

After my initial flurry of success, I started travelling further afield around London, collecting money from traders who owed Paul money from the past and had mistakenly believed that he'd forgotten the debt. Spitalfields Market was massive, and a market trader who owed Paul a couple of hundred quid could quite easily switch to another supplier and never be spotted. So if I didn't find the bloke I wanted on Paul's stand, that meant that I'd have to go out and find him. I got to know some of the other traders, and I'd tell them to look out for the blokes I needed to track down.

'Tell Frankie Owen I want to see him,' I'd say for instance, 'and if he doesn't come and see me then tell him I'll have to find him.' Usually they'd get the message and come to me sharply with the money that they owed.

I started keeping a book, and had reduced many of Paul's debts before long. But alongside those debtors who simply tried to dodge Paul and me at Spitalfields, there were also those who were prepared to go further afield to evade our clutches. There were three big markets around London at that time; alongside Spitalfields, there were also the big Nine Elms and Great Western markets. There were also a host of smaller ones, from Croydon to Epping. So if these blokes ran out of credit in one market, they'd go to another, attempting to avoid paying wherever they could.

So I had to travel about a fair amount in order to track down Paul's money. I was pretty successful. There were one or two who I had to chase a bit, and a couple of others who were a bit useful in a fight. If I knew that a bloke could hold his own in a punch-up with me, I wouldn't get physical, but would try to talk him around instead. After all, there was no point in having a fight and still not getting the money that Paul was owed. Despite drawing the occasional blank, however, I got quite good at my job, and was bring in a lot of money for Paul that he'd previously thought was lost. Paul rewarded me, paying me a wage, and employing me more often as a credit controller than a debt collector.

When I did have to collect, however, it often meant that I'd end up involved in a violent situation. On one of my assignments, I had to go after a guy who we used to call The Onion Man. It wasn't a particularly sophisticated nickname – we called him that because he only sold onions. He bought a lot of them from Paul but didn't pay for them. So I went over to his office on the other side of the market, broke in and turned it over: I literally turned his desk upside down, and smashed the office to pieces. But while I'd got to his property, I hadn't managed to get him, which meant that Paul was still out of pocket.

The Onion Man was very elusive, and I had to track him down to his home. I found out where he lived, in a village near Southend, and when I finally found it I was feeling pretty angry, which meant that I went further than I should have done. I set fire to his garage – burnt it to the ground – and eventually got hold of him. He was terrified, but I wasn't finished. I threatened him, bashed him up, and got some of the money out of him. I went away from there fully aware that, even by my standards, I'd gone too far.

Understandably, The Onion Man went to the police. A couple of days later, I was on the stand with

Paul, just standing there, when this copper walked up to me, taking me completely by surprise. Out of the corner of my eye I noticed that there was quite a crowd gathering. This guy gave me a real verbal battering, right in front of everyone, and he was swearing as well. If it had been anyone else, I would have ripped his head off, but there are rules in the East End, and one is that you never hit a man in uniform.

He really gave it to me with both barrels. 'You can't go around threatening people, Sunshine . . . I'm not having people on my beat being threatened by an ugly mug like yours . . .' Obviously, that's the clean version of what he said.

And I just stood there looking at him, and took it all, because he was in uniform. But I didn't leave it there.

A couple of hours later, I phoned the local police station, and asked to speak to this copper. I told him who I was; that I was the one he had given an earbashing to on the market earlier. He remembered me of course.

'How would you fancy meeting me, when you are off duty?' I asked him.

'What?' came the startled reply. He clearly wasn't expecting this.

I repeated my suggestion. 'How would you fancy meeting me after work, and talk to me like you did this morning, without your nice blue uniform on?'

'Why? You fancy your chances?'

'I do. If you want to forget you are a copper, come back and see me. Otherwise next time you come over, nick me, but don't ever talk to me like that again.'

In making that call I was trying to assert myself. I'd never dreamed that he would actually take me up on the offer. Yet that's exactly what he did. Later on that same day, this copper walked over to the stand, only this time he didn't have his uniform on. He was in plain clothes, wearing a bomber jacket.

Although I was angry over what he'd done to me in the market earlier on, I had a lot of respect for him now. He wasn't looking for my respect though – he was looking to teach me a lesson, and he obviously fancied his chances. And just the fact that he'd had the bottle to return showed me that he must be useful in a fight.

As he walked over to me, I didn't even hesitate. I went for him with full force – and it was clear from the lack of resistance that he put up that he had badly underestimated me. I threw him straight into a pallet of tomatoes, bashed him over the head a few times, and sent him to the floor. To his credit, not only did he dust himself down and walk away, but nothing more ever came of it.

The market had half-closed, so there were a few people around, but not many. Most of those who were there at that time were the market stallholders, not the general public, so there weren't too many people who saw what happened. That didn't matter, because the people who saw it were the people who I would have wanted to see it. All the owners in the market had watched me bash this copper up, and now they had further proof, if it were needed, that I was not to be messed with.

Before too long, most of the market and half of East London had heard that I had no fear of the police, and that I had beaten up this copper. My reputation was getting stronger and stronger.

As I planned to leave Jacqui for a third time, I realised that I would have to work to convince Donna that we could make a life together in Britain. She had begun to sort herself out, and only wanted to get involved with me if I could assure her that I wasn't going to drag her down. Like me, she'd stopped taking coke and had cleaned herself up. She'd got a job working in a department store which had branches all over the country, including one near her mum's house in Cardiff. After working there for a few months, she applied for a job internally, for a position as manager of the store in Wood

Green, London. It was a big step up for her, but they loved her attitude and gave her the job.

Now Donna was living locally again, and was earning enough money to support herself – a situation that we'd never been in before. Before long our affair had been rekindled, and I was trying to make her believe that my confusion was over, and that this time, I was really, honestly, leaving Jacqui for good. I knew the perfect way to persuade her.

'Buy a flat with me,' I suggested. 'Not rent: buy.'

'I can't afford that, Arthur,' she replied, 'and neither can you.'

She was right when she said I couldn't afford it, but she was wrong to think that it couldn't be done. I had a plan which, although illegal, would get us a flat of our own. Using the house I owned with Jacqui as equity, I knew that I'd be able to get a mortgage with Donna for another flat. All I had to do was forge Jacqui's signature.

8

The Guv'nor and Me

When the old Spitalfields Market closed and moved to a new site in Leytonstone, Paul moved down there and took the opportunity of expanding his business. He asked me to go with him, and offered me a decent, regular wage and even gave me a 'company car'. I earned £400 a week simply in my role as credit controller, and that didn't include the tips that I could often expect from punters. Because word had spread that I was a hard man, many people wanted to make sure that they stayed on my right side. When a trader came to the stand, Paul would sell them something, and then I would load it up onto pallets for the porters to take to the buyer's van. Most traders would slip me a five pound note, just to be 'friendly'.

Alongside all that, though, I was also still collecting debts for Paul and earning a decent percentage there, too. So when I brought in a big debt for Paul,

I could earn several thousand pounds on top of all the rest. Once again, having lost so much, I was back on my feet and earning well. I hadn't learned my lesson, though; just as before, I ploughed all my money back into my twin addictions – cocaine and Donna.

I set Donna up in the new flat, and everything was going well. We weren't living together – I was still with Jacqui as far as the postman was concerned – but we carried on our affair, and continued to meet up for what continued to be unfulfilling sexual encounters. I liked having her close by though, and as she pursued her new career, she was happy to be my mistress again.

For a while, we'd both managed to stop or slow down our drug intake. I was still using steroids for training and competition, but had no longer been snorting cocaine like it was thin air. That changed, however, with the move to the new market. Paul had started to get into it, and one of the new salesmen, a guy called Chris, was a big-time user. Suddenly, it seemed as if it was everywhere, all over the market. I wasn't strong enough to say no.

People knew my history with drugs, and soon the financial backhanders were being replaced by lines, and sometimes bags, of white powder. People would walk on to the stand and say, 'Here you go

Arthur, a little something for you.' So again, just like when I'd worked on the doors, I was simply being handed coke. I didn't have to go looking for it – I didn't even have to pay for it. Sometimes it was just a line or two, often it was a whole bag. Sometimes they'd give it to me just to get rid of it.

There was another, more sinister reason why they'd give it to me, however. A couple of people handed me 'bad coke', mixed with crushed glass or whatever, which was designed to kill me or put me in hospital. Somehow I managed to lead a charmed existence though. Because I had so much coke, I couldn't take it all, and before I could get to the bad coke that I'd been given, something happened. A bloke who knew that I had a big stash of drugs on the stand came over and nicked some of it, without my knowing. I only found out, days later, because the guy was seriously ill in hospital, having snorted my coke, which was mixed with glass. That fate was meant for me, yet hearing about it didn't slow me down. All this free coke was too good to be true, and I couldn't stop myself.

So I'd always have a bag of coke on me. I'd start work at one in the morning and snort a bit of coke, and that meant that I'd be running around like lightning. I used to sprint through the market chasing people who owed Paul money, and started to do more of the threatening part of the job right there on the market. And where previously I used to act with more caution around debtors who could handle themselves in a fight, now I didn't care who they were. There was one bloke who was a real lump: about 6' 6" and massive. I chased him across the market, caught him, and got him around the neck. But this guy was huge – much bigger and heavier than me – and he was shaking me around like a rag doll. Yet I didn't give up; I was like a Rottweiler attacking this bloke. In the end, I literally choked him to the ground, and then bashed him on the floor.

I didn't care what I did or who I started on. I was fired up by the coke, still on the steroids and in awesome physical shape. I believed that I was totally and utterly unstoppable. A theme that had woven itself through my entire life was just getting stronger and stronger: Arthur White was invincible.

One day I was over at Chapel Street Market in Islington. I'd gone to collect money from a bloke called Watkins who had started to run up some big debts with Paul. This bloke was bald and hated the fact, so would wear a cheese cutter hat. To get at him, I would regularly snatch the hat off his head, exposing his baldness. He hated that.

As I always did, I asked Watkins for the money Paul was owed, or at least a down payment, but he refused. I started to get a bit heavy with him, but then he said something which caused me to think twice: 'I'm a mate of Lenny McLean.' Lenny was an unlicensed boxing champion, well known as one of London's hardest men. He was a very serious geezer.

'You don't know Lenny,' I sneered, trying to work out if this was a bluff.

'I do. And if anyone gives me any grief, they'll have to answer to him.'

'That's interesting,' I replied. 'Because I know Lenny, too. Why don't I go and ask him about you?'

He stood his ground defiantly, but I could see in his eyes that this was not good news.

I used to train with Lenny at a gym in Bethnal Green Road. I had been introduced to him by my friend and fellow powerlifter Brian Jones. Brian was training him and he was getting huge. He was a big bloke anyway, and he was up to about nineteen stone in weight. He had a bit of a belly on him, but he was massive across the upper body. He spoke in a deep East End growl:

'Hello Arfur. Pleased to meet ya.'

I wasn't intimidated, but I knew that this was a serious bloke, and I treated him with due respect. Brian walked off and left us talking.

'Brian's a good bloke,' he said, not knowing that we were mates. 'Top powerlifter you know.'

Even though I wanted to treat Lenny with respect, I wasn't going to stand for this. Brian was nothing compared to me – I was a world champion. He was a broad guy, and very strong, but he wasn't in my league.

'You want to see a top powerlifter?' I asked. 'Let's get Brian back here, and I'll show you one.'

Lenny smirked and nodded. I called Brian back over, and challenged him to a competition, right in front of Lenny. Of course, Brian knew that he couldn't possibly beat me, but he was prepared to have a go. We started lifting, and right from the start, I was winning. Looking across, I could see that Lenny was getting upset. I was joking around because Brian and I were mates, but Lenny didn't know that and mistook my jibes for arrogance. After I'd beaten Brian, I walked away quietly, realising that my antics had not impressed Lenny. He didn't enjoy seeing his friend get beaten and apparently humiliated right in front of him.

I went across to the other side of the gym, and started doing a few sit-ups. Suddenly, as I was laying back on the mat, a huge shadow came over me and blocked out the light. It was Lenny. He'd clearly taken offence, and now I was about to find out what training with Brian had done for his muscles.

His huge face broke out into a broad grin. 'You've bin pulling me leg, ain't ya? I know who you are – you're Arfur White. You're a good powerlifter you are. Respect, son.' Brian had filled him in that I was a world and European champion. He shook my hand, and then I started to get to know him a bit better.

At forty, he was slightly past his prime, and not in the same sort of shape that saw him through his infamous battles with Roy 'Pretty Boy' Shaw. Yet Lenny was still involved in unlicensed fights and invited me to come down and watch. I went to see him fight this gypsy fella at the Earl Grey pub on the South Circular road. Lenny was so hyped up that he came into the ring spitting, and wearing just a pair of very thin weightlifting gloves and a pair of track-suit bottoms. He got into the ring, and the referee called them into the middle, but this gypsy bloke jumped up and head-butted Lenny before the fight could even get started. Lenny roared, bit his gloves off, and knocked the referee out of the way. He hit the gypsy just a couple of times, sending him crashing to the floor, then continued to pound him, even jumping on him. Then some more blokes jumped in the ring, trying to control Lenny. A battle ensued in the ring, and then it kicked off outside the ring – suddenly there was an all-out riot going on. As the sound of police sirens filled the air, I managed to slip away. There was no point rolling around on the floor with a bunch of drunks.

Lenny was supposed to have retired, but a few blokes – such as this gypsy fella – had been putting it around that they could beat him. In order to preserve his reputation, Lenny decided to come out of retirement, face these blokes in the ring and beat them. That's exactly what he did, and his need to train for the fights meant that we spent more time in the gym together, which is how we became friends.

With all of this still fresh in my mind, I knew that I would always need to be careful when Lenny's name was mentioned. Once this fella Watkins, who owed Paul money, had mentioned him as a friend, I realised that it would be sensible to at least check it out.

That evening, I went to see Lenny at his place of work, the Hippodrome nightclub in Leicester Square. He was the head doorman there, so he wasn't outside when I arrived. There was a huge lump of a man on the door, but in my coke-addled state, I was in no mood for talking.

'I've come to see Lenny,' I grunted.

'Who are you?' he asked, raising an arm.

'Never mind who I am,' I replied, pushing him out of the way with a hard shove, 'I'm a friend of Lenny's.'

Perhaps he was surprised by my strength, or perhaps he was just used to letting in hard-looking men who said they were friends of Lenny's. Either way, he didn't put up much resistance. I strolled into the club, and found my way into Lenny's office.

'Hello Arfur,' he said. He didn't seem at all bothered that I'd barged into his club.

'Hello Len. Sorry to drop in. I've got a bit of a problem.'

'Go on.'

'There's this bloke who I've got to go and collect from. Watkins his name is. He's put your name in the frame, said that if I leaned on him for money then you'd be having a little word. So I wanted to know how we stood.'

Lenny shrugged his massive shoulders. 'No problem Arfur. Nuffin' to do wiv me – never heard of the bloke. Give him a slap from me when you see him.'

'Fair enough Len, thanks.'

I turned to leave, but suddenly a thought struck me. This man was well known as one of the hardest men in London. In the ring he'd been known as 'The Guv'nor'; on the door he was nicknamed 'The King of Bouncers'. You could stop a fight on a dance floor just by mentioning his name. He could be a very useful ally.

I spun on my heels. 'Len,' I said, 'I've heard a few people put your name about in this game.'

'Oh yeah?'

'How would you like to come round with me tonight and see them? Help me sort out the debts, one way or another?'

Lenny thought for a moment. 'Yeah, alright. Pick me up from 'ere at midnight.'

We shook hands, and again I made for the door, but this time, it was Lenny who stopped me.

'Oh, and Arfur, that'll cost you a monkey.'

I smiled, nodded, and counted out five hundred quid. I walked out of there smiling though, because I knew I'd be collecting a lot more back now that Lenny McLean was on my firm.

Literally, every time I went out with Lenny it cost me five hundred quid – regardless of whether we collected or not. It would come out of my pocket, but I always knew I'd get it back, either from what I collected or from Paul, who was now even more proud. Now he could boast that two of London's most notorious men were on the street collecting for him. He might have been a soft touch when it came to credit, but when word got around about Lenny and me, the number of people looking to take advantage of him reduced greatly.

That night, when we went to pay Watkins a visit, he was his usual cocky self. He was still mouthing off to me that I'd better beware, and that Lenny was a mate of his. His face fell a million miles when my colleague stepped out of the shadows.

'Hello son,' said Lenny, grinning.

Watkins gulped. We didn't need to work hard on him in order to recover the full debt. But that's not to say we didn't teach him a little lesson, just to make sure he remembered not to use Lenny's name again.

I worked with Lenny for a couple of years. It wasn't every week – I couldn't afford to pay him that often – but it was regular, whenever I needed some extra muscle to get the job done. One afternoon, we went back to Spitalfields at about 2 o'clock, and the market was all closed up, with all the roller shutters down. Lenny had been flexing his muscles a fair amount that morning, and he'd begun to act a bit strangely. Just as when he was in the ring, violence tended to get his adrenaline pumping, and he'd start to behave like a hyperactive child.

'Arfur,' he said, 'I've got to do a bit of training. I've got to do some bag work.'

'Fair enough Len,' I replied. 'Let's head over to the gym. I'll help you train.'

'OK Arfur.'

I thought that we were about to leave, but Lenny started to stare at the shutters in front of him. He walked across to them, and slowly at first, began to punch them. I had no idea why he was doing it; he just kept putting his guard up, and hitting these shutters as if they were a punchbag. Then the blows got harder, and soon he was pounding at this metal with all his might. Crash! Crash! Crash! He wouldn't stop, and the noise was echoing all around the market. Blokes were coming out to see what was going on. Not only was Lenny hitting this shutter, he was also seriously denting it. If you'd been on the other side you'd have seen the thing bulging inwards as Lenny tried to fight his way through. I stepped back, and told everyone to just leave him until he calmed down. The market police turned up after a while, but when they saw who it was, they thought better of it and went away again. Eventually, as quickly as he'd begun, Lenny stopped punching the shutter, and stepped back.

'Come on Arfur,' he said. 'Let's go.'

And we did. No explanation was ever offered; that was simply the kind of thing that Lenny did, and exactly why he earned a reputation as a man to be feared.

One Monday morning we went out to collect some money from a bloke in Epping Market. Epping was about ten minutes from Loughton where I lived, and less than an hour from Spitalfields, but to Lenny, who rarely made it out of his patch of East and Central London, it was the other side of the world. We drove out through the forest, and it was eerily peaceful and quiet, both inside our car and out. We stopped at a coffee shop, owned by a mate of mine. As soon as he saw and recognised Lenny, he pleaded with me to take him somewhere else, because he was terrified of him. But I assured my friend that Lenny was harmless (as long as there were no metal shutters nearby), and managed to pacify him.

We sat at the front of the shop, just out on the street, and had a coffee together. Lenny was grinning. 'It's nice out here,' he said, unusually calm. 'Where are we?'

'This is Epping, Lenny.' I told him. 'This is Essex.'

'The old woman'd love it out 'ere. I think I'll buy 'er a place out here one day.'

'It's pretty steep out here, Len. You don't get too much for your money.'

'Ah, that don't matter. I'm gonna be rich soon anyway.'

'Oh yeah?'

'They're gonna make a film about me, Arfur.'

I wasn't sure about all that, but I certainly enjoyed the conversation. Here we were, two big lumps out on a debt collecting mission, and we're sitting in a coffee shop on the edge of the forest, having a drink and talking about the future. It must have been quite a sight for the other customers, especially when my mate brought out the coffee cups, and they were too small for Lenny's hands. He was used to a mug, not a dainty little cup like this, and he had hands like sledgehammers. He didn't get angry though – he was too peaceful. It was a side of Lenny I'd never seen before.

Of course, we had work to do. After we finished our drinks, we went to the market and I immediately spotted the fella we were after. We walked over, and he started giving me all the spiel about not being able to pay, even though I was absolutely sure that he had the money. Relaxed by our morning coffee, I was trying to be as nice as possible about it, but my partner in crime was displaying less patience. I looked across at Lenny, and I could see he was getting a bit agitated. Without warning, he put his hand under the front of the stall and tipped it over into the road. Huge volumes of fruit and veg went rolling across the road, and all the traffic had to stop. I stepped back, knowing that Lenny was now taking control of the situation. He picked this geezer up and turned him upside down, and started to shake him so that all his money fell out into the street. He was pleading with Lenny to put him down, but I could see that Lenny wasn't about to stop. He was going to ram his head into the road, and bash his skull in.

'Lenny!' I shouted, wanting to avoid a potential murder. 'Put him down!'

Thankfully, my words were enough to put Lenny off. He just threw him to the ground, and I picked up his money belt and motioned for us to walk away. We walked off with a couple of grand – enough to keep Paul happy for now. As we drove back through the forest, I could see that the old Lenny had returned, after his brief character change at the coffee shop.

'Sorry Arfur,' he said, 'I nearly lost it there listenin' to all the drivel comin' out of his mouth.' I had really thought that Lenny was going to tear this guy apart. It wouldn't have been out of keeping with the character of the man I knew.

It was funny walking around with Lenny. Not only did everyone back away when they saw us coming, also people that didn't know me thought that I was his brother. They thought I was just as dangerous and unpredictable as him, and so I earned the nickname 'Animal' around the markets. I was building a reputation off the back of his, although I didn't do that on purpose.

Lenny died in 1998. He was half right when he predicted that they'd one day make a film about him. After he got out of prison for his part in the death of a Hippodrome punter, he went on to have a short but successful acting career. Most famously, in the year of his death, he got cast as Barry the Baptist in Guy Ritchie's film *Lock Stock and Two Smoking Barrels*. If you watch that movie, and see Lenny in it, he isn't acting. That was just what Lenny McLean was like.

9

Falling Further

I was still utterly unable to commit to either of the women in my life. I had left both Jacqui and Donna several times over, but each time I had gone to settle with one I felt either guilt (with Donna) or claustrophobia (with Jacqui). For this reason, although I wanted to move in with Donna again, she wouldn't let me.

After I'd forged Jacqui's signature to obtain a mortgage, Donna and I had bought this flat in Waltham Abbey, again in Essex. It was newly built and immaculate. It was only a one bedroom apartment, but because it was the last flat left in the development, it was the show flat, which meant that they had really gone to town on making it look smart. And since it was full of all this pristine show furniture, I made the developer an offer and bought it all as well. Yet even though I'd gone to extreme lengths to get us this flat, Donna wouldn't let me move in. She said that if I did that, I'd just move in and out again, as I always did. After giving her the run around so often in the past, I couldn't really blame her for that. So Donna moved in, I stayed living with Jacqui, and we kept up our affair at arm's length. Once again, Jacqui had no idea that Donna was even in England, let alone in Essex.

With her career in retail taking off, Donna was happy. She now had her own flat, and a man who she could see whenever she wanted to. And, perhaps predictably, at this point she decided to stop wasting her life waiting for me to get my act together, and started getting involved with other blokes.

Strangely, considering all my other vices, I'd never really had a problem with alcohol. When I was working on the door I knew better than to drink because alcohol dulls the senses, and I didn't want to lose complete control. That probably sounds strange since I was always knocking back the coke, but I never considered that cocaine was reducing my control, it just intensified my concentration, and even if I lost it a bit when a fight kicked off, I would still always know what I was doing. And of course, the steroids gave me strength. Alcohol had a different kind of effect, however, and so I steered clear.

Around this time in 1992, however, I did hit the bottle in a big way on a couple of one-off occasions. If I was going to do it, I knew I'd need to be out of the East End because I couldn't risk running into an enemy when I was drunk. One night, I went over to a wine bar in Bexleyheath with a mate of mine, called Dean. He was a lot younger than me, only about eighteen or nineteen years old, and so everyone in the market thought he was my son.

We got absolutely hammered that night, but being irresponsible I still drove. I dropped Dean off at the Elephant and Castle, down in the South of London, and then headed back towards Leyton. I was absolutely paralytic, but I had convinced myself that I was going back to work.

What happened next proved that I was anything but fit to work, let alone drive. I felt myself slipping out of consciousness and the night turned into a complete blur. Hours later, I woke up on Westminster Bridge in the early hours of the morning. I had simply laid down on the side of the road, and blacked out. As I regained consciousness, I realised that my car was nowhere to be seen. I'd lost it. I was still pretty much out of my head and the sleep had only sobered me up slightly. I started to stagger back towards Spitalfields, or at least in the direction which I thought was best along the river

Thames, which I knew went east. I came to Tower Bridge, which is a fair distance away from Westminster, and saw my car, pulled up at the side of the road. Blind drunk, I'd hit the kerb, got out and left it there!

A few months after that, I went to Devon for a Saturday night out with my old friend Jim Duncan. It was another night of booze, and Jim was a much bigger drinker than Dean or me – he was a beer man. It wasn't a wild night but we drank a lot. I stayed the night with Jim, and rather than face the inevitable hangover, we decided to start drinking again on Sunday morning. This pattern continued throughout the day, until it was time for me to drive home. Once again I had to get back to work, and again I decided to drive home – this time a much greater distance – while drunk.

Just as before, I passed out, but this time I was at the wheel. Careering freely, I drove straight across a grassy roundabout, and miraculously, I didn't manage to hit anyone. I woke with a jolt and this time even I realised that it wasn't safe for me to be driving. I decided to stop as soon as I could and catch a bit of sleep. Ahead of me, I saw the tail-lights of a lorry, heading towards a built-up area of houses. I could hardly focus, and so I decided to just follow the lorry towards the houses, and then find somewhere to stop in this estate.

The lorry kept going, but after a while I realised that I was in a quiet road, and decided to get my head down for a nap. I pulled my van over, leaned the seat right back, and immediately fell asleep. I was just in my white company van, pulled over at the side of this road.

I can only describe what happened next as like being in a movie. The sound of a helicopter buzzed directly above me, and I was being blinded by scores of ultra-bright lights. There were voices shouting all around me, but I couldn't work out what they were saying. I sat my seat back up, and then heard a voice that I could make out: 'There's someone in the van!'

The doors were ripped open and two blokes grabbed me and wrenched me out of the van. They threw me to the floor and suddenly there was a gun to my head. As I looked around at all these snarling men, who were in uniform, and as the light now illuminated the 'houses' around me, I realised that this wasn't an estate at all. I'd parked in an army base!

There was a lot of swearing going on, I can tell you. I think they were angrier with the fact that I had managed to get inside without anyone seeing me, than they were about my actual presence there. The van was completely empty but they had a good look through it.

'I'm sorry,' I protested in slurred speech as the sergeant paused for breath. 'I just wanted to sleep. I pulled in here thinking it was a council estate.'

'What?' he screamed, absolutely incredulous.

Even I was slightly nervous here. I didn't have a chance against all these gun-toting soldiers. 'What's going to happen?' I asked, unusually timidly.

'What's going to happen?' he bellowed. 'We're going to stick you back in your van, airlift it onto Dartmoor, and blow you up!'

I was pretty sure that he was joking so I just looked at the floor.

'Get in your van, get out of here, and never, ever come back,' he said eventually. And not in those exact words . . .

They obviously didn't want anyone to find out about this, as it looked pretty bad on them from a security point of view. And even though I didn't tell anyone, word still got out. A few weeks later, Jim rang me and said: 'Tell me it wasn't you who pulled into the army base for a kip.'

The story had become a favourite in the local pubs – one of the soldiers must have let it slip. I was sure the sergeant wouldn't have been very impressed with that.

I gave up on my drinking phase at that point, but a little while later there was another act in my bizarre road movie. I was driving back from Cardiff, and this time I wasn't drunk but buzzing on coke. I managed to get as far as Hammersmith, just north of the river Thames. I drove across the Hammersmith flyover, heading back home in the early hours of the morning. At the time, I was training for a body-building competition that was about a month away which meant there was a cocktail of drugs in my body. As well as the coke I'd taken to keep myself awake, I was also on diuretics to keep the water levels in my body down.

I was in a sports car, which I'd borrowed, and so I was travelling pretty fast. I knew it would only take me twenty minutes to get to work from there, so I decided to pop a couple of diuretics so that they'd have worked by the time I got to the market. Obviously, diuretics make you pee, but I knew I could hold it for twenty minutes. The tablets didn't seem to work though, so I washed them down with a whole bottle of mineral water. Then, like an idiot, I threw the bottle out of my car window without first looking around. Predictably, there was a police car directly behind me.

The police sounded their horn and shouted to me to pull over. They were both women, and I'm sad to say I probably didn't quite treat them with the same respect as I might have done with two men.

'You've been drinking, sir,' one of them said.

'I haven't, love!' I actually hadn't. I was high as a kite on coke, though.

'Blow into this bag please.'

I completed the breathalyser test, but it came up negative. They weren't satisfied, and did another. Again, it was negative. They could clearly see that I wasn't right, but the test wouldn't convict me.

They called for back-up, and soon another car turned up – a patrol car. This time there were two men, and they brought their own breathalyser, presuming that the other one was malfunctioning. For a third time, the test showed up negative. They still didn't believe that I hadn't been drinking. It wasn't just the bottle I'd thrown – my driving had been all over the road. There is a way of tricking a breathalyser, and they were starting to assume that this was what I had done.

Because of the coke, my mouth was going into overdrive. I wasn't being stroppy, but I just couldn't stop speaking, further incriminating myself. Even as the words were coming out, a voice in my head was saying 'Shut up, Arthur!' Eventually, they got tired of listening to me.

'Right sir,' one of them said. 'We're going to need to take you back to the station.'

At which point, something happened. We'd been standing there at the side of the road for about twenty minutes. The diuretics had worked through my system, and now I was starting to get some serious bladder pain.

I asked if I could take a pee at the side of the road before we went, but the officer in charge said that I couldn't because I'd need to provide a urine sample back at the station. This was bad news for two reasons. Firstly, a urine sample would incriminate me for driving while high on cocaine, and secondly, the pain in my bladder was going to get an awful lot worse.

We got to Hammersmith police station, and by now I was limping from the pain. The officer gave me a small pot, and asked me to fill it. He didn't want me to take it into the toilet – I had to do it in the interview room where he could stand behind me and make sure I didn't tamper with the sample. I grabbed the pot, started doing what came naturally, and for a few moments felt a joyous rush of relief. But I'd taken diuretics, and so this pot was never going to big enough.

The pot was soon full, and soon everything is spilling over the top. Pee was starting to go all over the floor, and so I turned around and tried to hand him the pot.

'Give me another!' I demanded.

By now, he'd realised that I wasn't drunk. 'Get out of here!' he shouted.

He motioned dismissively at the pot, but in doing so, smacked it with the back of his hand. The pot spun in mid-air and my pee went all over him. He was livid now.

'Get out of here, you dirty dog!' he screamed.

I finally stopped peeing. 'How do I get back to my car? It's on Hammersmith flyover.'

'Walk,' he growled.

So I had to walk from Hammersmith police station back to the car. Had they tested that sample for drugs I'd have been in serious trouble. I had got away with it though, so I walked back to the car laughing my head off, got in and just drove back to work.

There was a company in the market called D.L. Bright. It was a wholesaler's firm. The proprietor would buy from different stands on the market and sell produce to the big hotels and restaurants all over London and the Home Counties. Doug Bright had fifty lorries and vans running twenty-four hours a day, six days a week, and his business would only close for twenty-four hours a week, from Saturday lunchtime to Sunday lunchtime. On Sunday afternoon it would open up again, the packers would make up the orders and load the lorries, and then the drivers would come in at three in the morning and deliver the stuff all over the place.

Doug used to come on to our stand and buy from Paul and he was a real character who was well liked. He enjoyed a bit of cocaine as well and was known for taking it, although not in the volumes that I was used to. He'd often hand me a bit of coke when he came onto the stand. Because he had a proper account, he'd pay Paul every month, but now and again I'd have to go over and ask him for a cheque. It was never a problem – he'd pay up straight away so I never got any commission on it – but during the meetings I got quite friendly with him, and also got to know the manager there, Earl Johnson. He was another character – he thought he was a bit handy because he could talk a bit, box well, and because he knew some people in the East End (and wouldn't hesitate to drop their names into a conversation). Because we'd got friendly, I often used to go over and have a cup of tea with Doug and Earl when I delivered some of their orders. Through 'contacts' who I didn't know much about, Earl used to 'get hold of stuff'. Sometimes it'd be clothing, sometimes televisions, cameras and the like. I never asked where it'd come from, but I was pretty sure he hadn't gone and bought it in the high street. Because of my reputation, he'd often give some of this stuff to me, just as an attempt to buy my friendship. When people fear you, everybody wants to be your friend.

During one of our tea breaks, Doug made me an offer which took me by surprise: 'Come and work for us, Arthur.'

'What?' I jolted. 'I don't know a cucumber from a tomato. What am I going to do here?'

Doug smiled. 'Earl could use some help in the warehouse, and besides, we've got a few problems that need sorting out.'

'What kind of problems?'

'Oh you know, the same sort of problems that Paul had, and that you sorted out for him. There's a few people who owe us money and I'd like to get that money back, if you get my meaning.'

I did, but out of loyalty to Paul I said that I'd have to think about it.

As it turned out, my mind was made up for me. I went back to our stand and within an hour had got myself into an argument with Paul's new business partner. I was sure that this bloke was dodgy, and my suspicions were further aroused when I saw him give a complete stranger twenty grand of Paul's credit. I told Paul that his partner was a con artist, and I said it right in front of both of them:

'Ask yourself, Paul, why is this geezer giving that much credit to someone you don't know?'

Paul shook his head, but his partner interrupted. 'Listen mate,' he said – and of course, no one talked to me like that – 'I'm Paul's partner now, and I make the decisions around here, not you. If you don't like it, you know where you can go.'

My eyes filled with rage, and I turned on him like a cobra: 'Listen son, I'll have your trousers down and smack you if you ever talk to me like that again.' He gulped hard, and stepped back.

I turned to Paul, told him again that he shouldn't be trusting this con artist, and said that I was finished. Paul thanked me for my hard work, and told me that there was no bitterness on his part. And as I walked across the market to accept a new job with Doug Bright, I did stop to worry that Paul could end up in trouble on account of the bloke. Sadly, it seems that I was proved right. As I write, Paul is doing seventeen years for money laundering, and his partner has managed to keep himself out of it.

Doug offered me £500 a week to be his assistant manager (with extra responsibility for debt control). He badly needed another manager to work alongside Earl as we had fifty lorry drivers and a hundred people working in the warehouse across two shifts. Because most of Doug's dealings were with big companies, usually all I'd have to do to collect a debt was phone their credit controllers and ask them to send us a cheque. The only real collecting that I had to do was as a result of Doug's drug-induced stupidity. Often, when he was high on coke, he'd do ridiculously generous deals for people, basically allowing them to walk away with crates of fruit and veg for free. That meant that I would have to go and track them down, and as nicely as possible, collect the money from them that they should have paid in the first place if Doug had quoted the real prices.

Working with Earl soon meant that I got involved in stolen gear. There were crates of champagne, vanloads of computers, cases full of suits. They were all coming into the market and they usually ended up at Earl's door – he had his finger in a thousand and one pies. We would always have a lorry in our car park, full of bent gear, which Earl would try to sell on whenever he got the chance. Working so closely with him, I couldn't really refuse to help him. By then I had become quite comfortable with criminal activity – where once it had seemed like I was only operating at the edges of the law, now crime was a part of my everyday life. Perhaps the main reason behind my failure to notice this shift was the amount of cocaine I was being given by people who came to the stand. It used to be that customers would slip me a line or two of coke to keep me on side, now people were coming to the stand just to hand it to me – and not just lines, bags of the stuff.

Fed by this limitless supply, my addiction grew to crazy proportions. In my office there was a small shelf, just inside a gap in the ceiling above where I sat. On that shelf, I hid a 2 lb sugar bag, but of course instead of having sugar in it, it was full of cocaine. I would go to work at midnight, and start my shift with a bowl of cornflakes – I would sprinkle the coke on my cereal in place of sugar. I'd put it in my coffee. Although it was incredibly dangerous to do so, I would even put it in other people's coffee, just as a joke. I found it funny to watch them running around the market like demented idiots, not knowing what they were doing.

As I was getting so much – more than even I could use – and it was all free, I would use it recklessly, and without really thinking. I would take more of it than I had ever taken before, because now I didn't have to worry about its cost. And of course, I didn't worry about what it was doing to my body – my invincibility complex told me that I was so physically fit that my body was just absorbing the cocaine and processing it harmlessly. So if I was going training, even if it was just for a light workout, I would take a wad of coke. I'm not lying, I would have a couple of teaspoons full of it every time.

Throughout the years that I worked at Spitalfields, I came across a lot of people whose lives had been ruined by one thing or another. Doug, for instance, had a multimillion pound business, but because he also had a big coke habit, he ended up nearly losing his wife. There were plenty of other blokes down there whose lives had been screwed up, and whose marriages had broken up because of drink and drugs. Then there were the so-called hard nuts, who got themselves messed up because of crime and violence. Then there were people like me, who had managed to get themselves tangled up in both.

There were people all around me who weren't in a good place – it certainly wasn't just me. But even though I could see what was happening to all these people, even though I could see their lives careering off the rails, I still allowed my life to go the same way. Now I inhabited a world where it was normal to have stolen goods in your front room, where it was easier to talk about bashing someone than it was to talk about loving someone. I was totally embedded in this world of drugs, violence, crime and evil, and it was crippling me.

I had always maintained, since the very first time I'd taken cocaine and steroids, that I would remain in control. I never referred to my drug use as addictive, because that would have implied that I wasn't in charge of it. But the truth was that from quite early on, I was completely addicted. I needed that stuff to get me through the day, even if I couldn't admit it. Since then it had got much, much worse – I was putting the stuff in my coffee, and on my corn-flakes! If I'd ever been in control at all, I certainly wasn't now. Now, the drugs were controlling me.

10

Rock Bottom

Donna had grown tired of me, and although I wasn't sure, I thought she was probably seeing someone else (at the flat which I was still paying for). We barely saw each other any more, but this time, I didn't go back to Jacqui. I'd been living with my mum for a while, but as a forty-something world powerlifting champion, that really didn't do my image much good, so I needed somewhere else to stay.

I knew that my brother owned a bedsit in Leyton, just a stone's throw from Spitalfields Market. It was in an ideal location for me, so I asked him if I could rent it. He agreed, for a fair price, so I moved into it with what little possessions I still had.

The bedsit was almost directly opposite Leyton Orient Football Ground, but it wasn't full of football fans. In fact, everybody else in the block was an old age pensioner. Although it was very clean and tidy, I instinctively realised very early on that this just wasn't the right place for me to be. I hated Leyton, even the walk around the corner to the local Chinese takeaway – which I used most nights – was horrible. The first night that I moved in I sat in this poky little room and picked at my chicken chow mein. Just a few years earlier, I'd lived in a huge family home in a nice part of Essex. I'd driven a Jag, owned a successful business and had a perfect family. How was it possible that now, just a few years on, I was working as a hired thug, scoffing takeaway in a tiny bedsit with barely a true friend in the world?

Living in this nasty area, in this tiny little room, made me very paranoid. Because I'd fallen so far, I now started to believe that everyone was out to get me. One night I was walking back from the Chinese takeaway with my little white bag, same as every night, and I heard footsteps running up behind me. Instinctively, I turned, swinging the bag, and hit this fella full in the face with it. As he stepped back, stunned, I heaved a couple of big punches into his stomach and head, and knocked him out cold on the floor. I stood over him, growling, and then noticed a bus, passing us in the road. It stopped just ahead. This was just a harmless little guy who'd been running to catch his bus, and I'd laid him out in the street. I realised that I was living right on the edge of sanity now.

The drugs were really beginning to leave their mark on me. Apart from my little cartons of Chinese food, I didn't eat much, as the coke and steroids were curbing my appetite. Just as many smokers are thin because their addiction removes their appetite, so drug users can find the same thing. The only reason I ever went to get food was because it meant I had a reason to go out into the normal world and meet a few people who weren't into drugs, guns or stolen goods. The little man who worked in the takeaway was my last link to civilised society.

The other big effect on my body involved my eyes. At one time, I hadn't slept for four or five days. I was pounding the coke into my body, working long hours at the market and also doing a bit of collecting, and so I hadn't had much of a chance to rest my head. When I eventually came home to get some sleep, I'd been unable to persuade my body to comply. I was massively overtired and I just couldn't get to sleep. The thing is, when you've been awake for five days straight, your eyes begin to ache. The best analogy is this: if you can imagine walking for four or five days without stopping, then your legs are going to ache. It's exactly the same with the eyes; there is an important muscle behind each eye, and because I hadn't slept, they hadn't rested.

I was in agony, and I was desperate. I was by now deeply depressed, shattered by the realisation of how I'd ruined my life. I lay there in the darkness, with a cold towel draped over my eyes, trying to take the pain away, and for the first time, my thoughts turned to the unthinkable. With my eyes still closed, I ran my fingers along the sheaf of the knife that, even when I was in bed, I kept strapped to my forearm. My other hand moved to my throat. One quick cut in the right place, I thought, and I could make all this pain go away. For the first time in my life, I was contemplating suicide.

I decided that I needed a holiday. Life at the market was so-so – although I was racking up an increasing number of enemies – but it was living in the bedsit that was really getting me down. I called Donna and asked her if she wanted to get away together – just for a week or so. As usual, I offered to pay, so she agreed. I chose Tenerife, which was ironic, because Donna's mother was on holiday there at the exact same time. Obviously this wasn't intentional; after all we'd been through, and the amount of times she'd been left to pick up the pieces, I was hardly this woman's favourite person. Donna assured me that it wouldn't be a problem though – she would go and meet her mum everyday, but not tell her that she was there with me.

We flew out a few days later, and just as planned, Donna disappeared each day to see her mum, who thought Donna had come out with some friends. Each day, I would sit on the beach and sunbathe, perhaps with an English paper to keep me company. The first day, this all worked well. The hot sun was a world away from the bleak East End that I'd left behind, and I finally managed to get some much-needed rest. Donna returned from seeing her mum, we went out for a meal, and for one of the only times in our relationship, it seemed that we were truly enjoying one another's com-pany.

That didn't last long, however. The very next day, as Donna left to meet her mum, and I settled on the beach once more, I found that my head was suddenly less clear. And once again, in the middle of this romantic holiday with Donna, I found that my thoughts turned back to Jacqui. I couldn't believe it: I was missing Jacqui.

A few weeks earlier, I'd been to visit my old friend Jim Duncan at his home in Devon. He and I were talking about our lives and he said something which really hit the nail on the head. Jim had never met Donna. I told him that Jacqui and I had split up permanently, but even then he had known that Donna and I would never get it right.

'It's over,' I told him. 'My marriage is finished. I can't keep going backwards and forwards – it ain't fair on Donna, and it certainly ain't fair on my Jacq. I've got to move on now, forget about my Jacq. I've got to think about sorting things out with Donna – she's my future.'

He smiled and shook his head. 'No Arthur, I'm not sure she is.'

'No,' I protested, 'she is. I've made up my mind.'

'Then why aren't you over Jacqui?'

'I am!'

I didn't see where Jim was coming from, but I wasn't angry – he was one of the only people I could still call a friend. 'What are you getting at Jim?'

'Don't you realise that you still talk about her as "My Jacq"? Whenever you talk, it's always "My Jacq this" and "My Jacq that". You're not over her Arthur.'

As soon as he said those words, I knew he was absolutely right. The bond I had with Jacqui was so deep that not even the events of the last three years had been able to destroy it completely. And yet I knew that there was no way that Jacqui would consider taking me back again after all I'd done, and all the times I'd left her. It just wasn't conceivable that anyone could be that forgiving.

So as I lay on that beach, unable to get Jacqui out of my head, this enormous cloud of depression descended on me. I realised that while she had once vowed to give herself to me completely, the woman I truly loved was now completely inaccessible. I had abused those marital vows almost beyond belief. Now there was no way back. And sitting there, coming to the realisation that the thing I wanted most in world was the one thing I could never have – and that I had thrown that very same thing away – I suddenly experienced a stark change of mood. When I had got up that morning, I had only thought of sunbathing, swimming, good food and (of course) a bagful of cocaine. Now, all those things had been forced out of my mind by one thought – one tremendous primal urge. I wanted to end it all. I wanted to kill myself.

That night, I couldn't sleep. So while Donna, who was sleeping off a large meal and a couple of bottles of wine, lay still, I crept out of bed and went for a walk along the beach at 4 o'clock in the morning. I couldn't stop thinking about the awful things that had earlier been going through my mind. I couldn't shake the desire to kill myself – it just seemed like the only way out of my problems.

As I looked out at the glistening moonlit waters, I had a morbid idea. I stopped, turned out to sea and, staring a thousand yards into the distance, I just began to put one foot in front of the other. I walked all the way down the beach and into the sea. Within thirty seconds I was up to my knees. After a minute I was up to my chest. Still I kept walking. I knew that I was a terrible swimmer, and so I knew that if I could just get far enough out to sea, I'd never be able to get back. There was certainly no one around to save me. Drowning seemed like an easy way out; it might be hell for a couple of minutes, but it'd be over soon enough.

Then, suddenly, as I reached the point when only my head was above water, I heard a voice, talking to me as if it was right there in the water: 'You cannot take your own life, my son.'

I was stunned. There was no one else around. Apart from the splashes that I was creating, the rest of the waters were utterly still. Yet as I looked again, I thought I could make out a face – in one way close by, and in another, far away. It wasn't a person, and yet it was a human face. I can only describe it as supernatural. I was trembling – something which I didn't normally do. Not only was I in the middle of a suicide attempt – now I was being unexpectedly interrupted by some sort of apparition.

'W-who . . . who are you?' I spluttered.

'I'm your father,' the voice replied.

It certainly wasn't the face or voice of my old man.

'You're not my dad!' I shouted desperately. 'My dad's been dead for years!'

And as soon as I'd said those words, this thing had disappeared, just as quickly as it had come.

I staggered back towards the beach. I had lost the appetite for this now. Utterly shattered, I threw myself onto the sand, and collapsed with my head in my hands.

'Arthur, you're bleedin' losing it now, mate,' I moaned to myself. Now I was hallucinating – I'd really lost the plot. Before I had a chance to let out the tears that were beginning to well up inside me, however, I realised that I was no longer alone. For a moment I worried that this would be yet another hallucination, that I had gone mad and would be left seeing things for the rest of my life. But this time there were no ghostly figures beside me.

This little old fella, probably in his early sixties, had come over to see what was wrong with me. He was wearing an old cap and a reefer jacket, and he looked like the sailor on the front of an old packet of Players cigarettes.

'You alright, son?' he asked.

'Not really,' I replied. I didn't make a habit of making myself vulnerable to complete strangers (or even to my friends), but these were extraordinary circumstances. I was sitting on a beach in Tenerife at four in the morning, and I had just had my suicide attempt interrupted by a voice from beyond.

'What's wrong with you, son?'

'I think I'm losing it,' I said, looking down at the beach. 'I'm seeing things. Truth be told, I'm not even sure if you're real or not.'

The old man chuckled. 'You look like a fit man,' he said.

'I'm a powerlifter.'

He raised an eyebrow. He seemed to know a bit about lifting. 'You found a gym here?' he asked.

'No. I could do with a workout though – to take my mind off a few things.'

'There's a gym under the hotel over there,' he said, indicating in the direction of the very building that I was staying in. 'Maybe you just need to get back to what you know.'

I told him that I hadn't known about the gym and thanked him. He smiled and walked away, and as I considered whether to make another attempt on my life, I realised that the moment had passed. So although that conversation hadn't been particularly interesting or revelatory, it had possibly just saved my life. I hauled myself to my feet, and back to my hotel, making a mental note on the way to give the gym a try in the morning.

The next day, when Donna went off to see her mum, I went down to check out this gym. It was fairly well equipped, so I pulled on my kit and began to train – for once, drug free. As I was working out, this British bloke who worked there came up to me and struck up a conversation. He could see that I was pushing some huge weights by normal gym standards so I told him who I was, and about all the titles that I'd won. He asked if he could take some pictures for the wall, and was very pleased when I agreed.

I asked him about himself, and he explained that he was a former naval officer, who was now a minister of religion. He worked as a chaplain in the local area, and told me that he was getting ready to sell up and move back to England.

'I'm just waiting to hear from "him upstairs",' he joked. At the time, I assumed he was talking about the hotel manager.

I told him a little bit about what had happened on the previous evening – he was a good listener. He gave me a little pep talk, told me that it was a good thing I'd run into that old geezer on the beach, that it was understandable that I was feeling depressed with all that was going on at home, but that suicide was the wrong answer.

'You can't go killing the World Powerlifting Champion,' he joked.

He gave me his card, and told me to give him a call if I ever wanted to talk with someone about these things. Then, as he left me to continue my workout, he just said a few simple words: 'There's more than one way out of this, Arthur.'

The year 1992 was coming to an end. It had been four years since I'd started my descent, and I was very weary. I survived the Tenerife holiday, mainly thanks to the old man on the beach and the chaplain in the gym, but only just. My thoughts still often turned to suicide, especially late at night in the bed-sit. This chaplain had talked of 'another way out', but that had been easy for him to say. He didn't have to wake up every morning, look in the mirror and see my face looking guiltily back. I could hardly look myself in the eye any more. That meant that even in moments of elation, I would soon find myself tumbling back into depression.

In November, I competed in the WPC World Championships in Stone, Staffordshire. I had already won the European and the British titles that year, and I was looking to make it a hat trick after my second-place finish in the 1991 Worlds. I was obviously bang on the gear, and the coke, but as I've already explained, that didn't matter to the WPC. It did matter to my emotional state though, so all through the event I was suffering from intense inner turmoil. In the context of the competition, I think that's perhaps what drove me on – I won the title hands down, and I also broke all kinds of British, European and World records. When I stopped lifting, however, my emotional state no longer had a positive effect.

After the event had finished, I went up to my hotel room to get changed. I was going to hit the town with the other lifters, as we always did after a big event. You can imagine what kind of havoc we caused: no nightclub owner would have wanted to see a band of coke-head weightlifters heading for his door. Tonight, though, I really didn't feel like partying. As I left the room, I caught my own eye in the mirror, I didn't feel the glory of a crushing victory in the sport I'd trained my whole life for. I felt shame.

I put plenty of coke and booze into my body in an attempt to improve my mood. For a while it worked – in the nightclub I temporarily forgot my troubles – even pushing a professional dancer off his podium so that I could get up there and give it my John Travolta act. But as the night wore on, I soon found myself deflating again. Coke just didn't have the same transforming effect on me that it used to – I'd just taken too much of the stuff.

I stumbled into my hotel room at four in the morning, alone and with a very sore head. Again, I caught my reflection in the mirror, and again all the terrible memories of how I'd screwed up my life came flooding back. This was supposed to be the greatest moment of victory in my life, and yet not only was my wife not with me, we weren't even talking any more. Sitting down in an armchair, and sobering up fast, I realised that yet another kind of pain was announcing itself. I was used to aching after an event, but this was different – this was my chest. I didn't need a doctor to tell me that the wheels were coming off. I'd been pumping junk into my body for years – there was always going to be a pay-off eventually.

For perhaps the first time in my life, I no longer felt invincible. In fact, I felt positively weak. I was the newly crowned World Powerlifting Champion, and yet tears were running down my cheeks. My life was in pieces, my body was starting to break down – there was surely only one way out now. Bending down, I unstrapped the twelve-inch knife that I'd earlier attached to my leg. I put it on the table in front of me and just looked at it. The blade glistened invitingly at me – almost like a wink.

When you take a lot of cocaine, the highs can take you really high, but the lows are just as low. You can go on a massive downer, and it can happen in the middle of a period of elation. This time, the downer was as big as it had ever been. Clutching my chest in agony now, I openly sobbed. All I wanted was for this to end, so that Jacqui could get on with her life.

Yet when it came to it, I just couldn't go through with suicide. I couldn't take the blade on the short journey needed to sever an artery and end my life. I can't put my finger on exactly why, but part of the reason was that the words of that chaplain from Tenerife were still in the back of my mind: 'There's more than one way out of this, Arthur.'

I had no idea what it meant, but it was a tiny seed of hope in all the agony and gloom, and it was enough to put me off. Exhausted, I hauled my battered frame across to the bed, and turned out the light.

When I got back to London, I told my friend Jim Duncan about the pains I was having.

'Arthur, you've got to get that checked out!' he said, concerned.

'I'm not going to see a doctor – he'll just say it's because I'm taking the gear,' I snorted.

'No, I've got a good doctor who will see you. He's a sportsman and he understands about steroids and

other drugs. He's not involved in it, but he understands.'

'I'm not sure . . .'

'Arthur, you've got heart problems. This is a serious thing.'

Reluctantly, I went to the address he gave me, in
London's famous Harley Street, and saw this doctor. He X-rayed my chest when I arrived, then asked
me to sit in the reception to wait for the results. He
called me back in a short while later.

He said very little, but put the X-rays up on the
screen for me to look at. The X-rays showed my
heart, although I only knew that because he told me
so. It didn't look like a heart – it looked like a football. It was certainly the size of a football, and it
was almost round. There were lines across it, that
looked like scoring. But the lines weren't cuts, they
were stretch marks. My heart had stretch marks on
it.

'I've got to be honest with you, Mr White,' he said
gravely. 'I've never seen anything like this in my
whole career. We both know that whatever you're
taking has caused this, but I'm actually frightened
to tell you to stop, because if you stop working your
heart like this suddenly, the shock could kill you.
On the other hand, I know if you continue, you will
certainly die. I don't know what to say.'

I was stunned. 'So what am I supposed to do?' I asked.

'Well, what on earth have you been taking?'

I didn't hold back. 'Steroids, coke, bit of speed. You know, bit of this and that.'

He tried not to look shocked. 'Well then, you've got to start cutting it down. It's killing you, Mr White.'

There was no way I was going to stop. I pulled the X-ray off the screen, screwed it up in my hand, and walked out.

When I spoke to Jim, who'd obviously talked to his doctor friend, I got more of the diagnosis. Steroid use forms fat particles in the blood, which harden around the arteries. It's fairly harmless if you're taking the drug for medicinal use, but I was using the gear abusively and excessively, so my arteries were hardening right up. At the same time as taking all these steroids though, I'd been taking cocaine. Cocaine has an effect on your heart which makes it beat faster, trying to pump the blood around the body quicker than it should. Put those two factors together, and you're placing your heart at tremendous risk, and sooner or later you are going to have a heart attack.

During my training and competing career, I've known nine blokes die of this kind of combined steroid and cocaine abuse. Eventually, their hearts have just exploded. The youngest of them, Ben Franks, was just twenty-one when he died. He was a huge man, who had the potential to become the World's Strongest Man. Another, and the most famous, was an Icelandic fella called Jan Arne Gudjonnson who won that competition, and was a very good friend of mine. He was thirty-two when he died, and when they did a post mortem on him they found that he was full of those same two drugs, steroids and cocaine. And even though I knew all of this, I didn't stop. I was killing myself, and I knew it.

It was January, and I had just endured the worst Christmas of my life. I wasn't with Donna – she was definitely seeing someone else now – and I didn't have the front to try to get back with Jacqui, even though that was what I wanted badly. What should have been a happy family time – and for twenty years had been exactly that – was just me, and a bag of Chinese, trying to stave off suicidal thoughts. And of course, my chest was killing me, quite literally. I really didn't get into the Christmas spirit that year, although I did half-make a New Year's resolution that I'd try not to waste any more of my time with Donna.

It didn't last very long. Very early one Sunday morning – it might have been 1 a.m. – I heard a knock at the door. It was one of Donna's mates saying that Donna had been beaten up by this bloke in Tottenham, and asking if I could help. Donna was still dealing drugs for this gang in Basildon, and one of her customers had decided not to pay. When she got angry with him, he'd hit her, and hard. He knocked her out cold on the pavement and left here there. I went outside, and saw Donna there, sitting in a car. She was very upset because she was now in trouble with these guys in Basildon if she couldn't give them their money.

Although I'd just promised myself that I'd no longer be involved in her life, I just couldn't turn my back on her at this point. I only said three words to her: 'I'll sort it.'

I ran back upstairs, and got dressed in a singlet, tracksuit bottoms and a pair of trainers – even though it was the middle of winter! The singlet obviously exposed my arms, meaning that as I emerged, I had my diver's knife in view for all the world to see. I jumped in my car and followed the girls over to a club in White Hart Lane, near the Tottenham Hotspur football ground. Donna knew that this bloke was inside. We got there just after closing time, as everyone was pouring out of the club into the street. I wondered if I'd missed the bloke I was looking for, but Donna spotted him and pointed him out to me. As I looked at him, he saw me and instantly realised what was going on. He started running instantaneously.

At school I'd been a champion sprinter – now I was much bulkier and a lot slower, but I could still sprint like a puma. I cornered him in the car park, and ended up in the middle of a childlike game – he was one side of a van, I was the other – and he kept managing to avoid me as I chased him in circles. I soon grew tired of this, and seeing that this van had a roof rack, grabbed it and vaulted over the van. I was in awesome shape then (I wish I could do that now!) and he was shocked to see me come flying over this van towards him. I landed almost on top of him, thumped him in the back, and sent him sprawling to the ground. As he fell, I pulled out my knife and stabbed him twice, deliberately in places that I knew wouldn't kill him. I could have easily stopped there, but by now I had worked myself up into a frenzy, and I wanted to teach him a lesson that he would never forget. Taking his head in my vice-like grip, I turned my knife to his ear and began sawing it off. I was part way through this grisly process when a loud voice, right by my ear, shouted: 'Arthur, stop!'

I couldn't identify it – it was too deep to be Donna or any of her mates – but it was enough to make me stop and realise what was going on. I stood up and looked down on this guy, half-dead on the tarmac. Then I looked up, and noticed that a hefty crowd of mainly men was heading towards us. None of them were yet close enough to have been the owner of that voice, however. In fact, there was no one within fifty feet of us.

As I saw this mob, I thought that I was going to get seriously hurt. I was well out of my own manor, I knew no one, and I'd just stabbed one of theirs. For all I knew, he could have been a well-connected local heavy. Stooping for a moment, I went through my victim's pockets, took all the money he had, and then just started walking towards the mob, head down and knife in hand. To my surprise, the crowd just parted and let me walk through. I have no idea why.

I went back to Donna at the front of the club, and handed her the money that I had taken. Saying nothing, I simply got into my car and drove off. I was buzzing so much from the coke, the steroids and the experience that I knew there was no point in returning home to sleep, so I just went straight to work. That night, people noticed that I was unusually quiet.

11

Life or Death

I had grown sick of living alone in the bedsit. I hated the area, I hated the loneliness and I hated having to live in such a cramped little space when I was paying two mortgages elsewhere. I decided that, after all, moving in with my mum wouldn't be such a terrible idea. I had a good relationship with my mum, although she didn't know I was into drugs. She knew I had a few fights, though, because the evidence of that was sometimes impossible to hide from her. She also knew about Donna, and had even met her a couple of times. She didn't like her of course, because she loved Jacqui like a daughter, but she had tolerated her when she'd been around. So considering that she knew all these things about me, and still loved me as a son, that made her the best person – perhaps the only person – for me to live with.

My mum's house was literally around the corner from my old house in Loughton, where Jacqui and the kids still lived. Mum still saw them regularly, which meant that it started to become easier for me to get in touch with Jacqui. Another good reason for the move was the fact that I didn't have to pay her any rent – a good thing considering my two mortgages and the amount I was still spending on hard living and steroids. I'd often blow £40 or £50 going out for a meal, so although I was earning good money, I rarely had much of it in my wallet.

In total, over the years, I'd left Jacqui and returned to her seven times. Sometimes I'd disappeared for a few nights, other times – when Donna and I made our more serious attempts at living together – it was a few weeks. I guess I'd always viewed her with a certain lack of respect because she'd always welcomed me back; in a way I was throwing her unconditional love for me straight back in her face. So it came as something of a shock to me when I realised that she was starting to sort out a bit of a life for herself, and beginning to move on from me. She'd got a job at another building company, and she'd started to go to a local church with Emma.

At some point in the previous year, when I was still living at home, Emma told me she'd found God. Or, as she put it, 'become a born-again Christian'. It was all I could do not to laugh in her face when she said that. And when she told me 'I believe in Jesus,' I could no longer hold back:

'Sorry sweetheart, but that's a load of old rubbish,' I said, and watched her face fall.

Two months later I walked out on them again. I later found out that she wrote a long and emotional page in her diary that night, including the words: 'I become a Christian, my dad leaves – what's going on?'

Yet my leaving didn't cause Emma to lose her faith. Instead, it made her stronger. She was a very strong young woman, but I guess she'd had to be with a dad like me. In some of the darkest moments, it was Emma who would be straightest with me. She never stopped loving her dad, but she hated what I was doing to them. She grew up fast, and I was very proud of her, even at a distance. Sometimes, after a violent brawl or a particularly heavy session with the coke, I wondered how on earth she could have come from me. I thought that about both my kids. James was growing up to be a great young lad, too, and was showing no signs of replicating his dad's many flaws.

It was even harder for me to watch these kids growing up from such a short distance now, living at my mum's. And suddenly there were all these other men in Jacqui's life, from work and the church. Having always been the perpetrator of adultery in our marriage, and having never even seen Jacqui with a bloke who wasn't either a mate of mine or related to her, this came as a bit of shock. The boot was on the other foot now, and I didn't like it. I started to feel jealous, wondering if I was about to lose my wife to another man.

I resolved once more that I would completely put Donna out of my life and focus on trying to get my family back together. And once again, as I made that decision, Donna came calling.

This time, she rang me in tears, asking if we could meet. I knew the answer to that one it was easy: 'I don't think that's a good idea, Donna. Sorry.'

'Arthur, I'm pregnant.'

Immediately, my good intentions went out of the window, and I knew I had to meet her. I was certain that the baby wasn't mine – we hadn't slept together for months, and anyway, I'd had a vasectomy back in 1982, and the two attempts I'd had at reversing the operation when I was with Donna had gone painfully wrong. I wanted to know who the father was though – and even if I had no right to be, I was still angry. The news left a fair dent in my ego: now I knew for sure that Donna was seeing other men.

We met up, and she told me that she had already made up her mind to have an abortion, so I didn't try to talk her out of it. She wouldn't tell me who the father was, she wasn't prepared to tell anyone that, because she didn't want him to ever find out what had happened. I tried to reassure her that this was her decision to make, but at the back of my mind I did feel a tiny bit sorry for this bloke, whoever he was.

Donna needed help if she was going to go through with the abortion, and I was the only person she could turn to. I took her to a clinic in Buckhurst Hill, Essex, and at the end of the operation I picked her up and took her home again. I was so kind to her in fact that her feelings for me started to rekindle. She realised that deep down, despite all the rubbish that had gone on between us, she still wanted to be with me. She had seen the side of me that I usually kept hidden by then, the side of me that had caused her to fall for me in the first place. Despite my resolution, we started talking again.

Almost the same day, the lines of communication opened up between Jacqui and me. She came round to visit my mum quite regularly, and each time she did, we exchanged a few more words. Eventually, she began to believe that I was sorting my life out – that I had finally finished with Donna, and that I had given up on the drugs. And to be fair, that wasn't all that far from the truth. Donna and I hadn't spoken for a while until the abortion, and I was taking less of both the steroids and the coke because of the chest pains, which I was still suffering from.

Day by day, we inched closer together. She was badly burned from what I'd done to her, but there was no doubt that she still loved me. What needed to happen was for trust to build up between us, and that would take time. But just as this was happening, and I was telling her that I was a changed man and would never deceive her again, Donna let me know that she was also leaving the door open. I had a decision to make, and despite all the opportunities I'd been given to learn a lesson, I got it wrong again. I should have just told Donna to leave me alone, explained to her that I loved my family and still wanted to sort things out with them. But I wasn't capable of truly changing. My lusts still ruled my head, and Donna was still a stunner.

So as I was talking with Jacqui about resurrecting our marriage, I also began talking with Donna about resurrecting our affair. At first I tried not to, but Donna was too good at temptation. She told me that she really loved me, that she needed me, that I cared for her like no one else. My oversized heart melted, and I agreed that we'd give it another try.

It was 20 February 1993. I was at my mum's house, and I was in my bedroom, talking on the phone to

Donna. Jacqui came round to see me, to ask me if I wanted to come over for dinner, and my mum let her in. I didn't know she was there – I didn't hear her come in; I didn't hear her come up the stairs. She heard me though. She heard that I was on the phone, so just waited outside the door and listened for a moment.

'Don't worry,' she heard me say. 'I love you. I want to be with you.' And then the killer blow: 'No . . . don't worry about that. It's finished between Jacq and me.'

Jacqui stormed through the door, grabbed the phone out of my hand, and slammed down the receiver.

'How could you?' she screamed. 'How could you?'

I was speechless. I had been caught red-handed.

'That's it, Arthur,' she said. 'That's it. We're finished. And this time, we're finished for good.'

As soon as she walked away, I knew she meant it. My marriage was over.

Minutes later, Donna called back.

'Arthur, who was that?' she asked. 'Who was that screaming?'

I was shell-shocked from what had just happened. I didn't have the mental capacity to lie any more. So I told her the truth: 'It was Jacqui. She came round here to see me, and she heard me on the phone to you.'

Her tone changed. 'Jacqui? What was Jacqui doing round at your mum's?'

Again, I didn't have the strength to lie. I told her everything – that while we'd been talking about getting back together, I'd been having the same conversation with Jacqui.

Donna was livid. All those feelings that she'd started having for me again simply evaporated. We had a serious row on the phone, and by the time we'd hung up, it was over. After seven unsuccessful attempts to get our relationship off the ground, we finally gave up on it.

That morning, I'd had a wife and a mistress, both of whom wanted to be with me. By the end of the day, I'd lost them both, for good. As I sat on the bed, head in hands, any grief for the loss of Donna barely registered. All I could think about was Jacqui, and how this time, I'd really lost her. Right then, I knew that I was really on my own for the first time. Even in the light of years of East End violence, it was probably the hardest blow I had ever taken.

Everything in my life had gone wrong. I'd lost my wife, my children, my house, my car, my business . . . Everything had slipped through my grasp. I was still addicted to at least two kinds of drugs, and the pain in my chest was sure to kill me eventually. There were plenty of men in London who I'd made serious enemies of, and they would happily have taken my life. It is no exaggeration to say that as I saw it, my life was literally over. And with that thought, I realised that it was time to speed up the process. The chaplain in that Tenerife gym had been mistaken, there was no other way out.

I decided that I would kill myself, and I decided that this time I would do it properly. At five in the morning, while London slept, I went into a corner shop not far from Spitalfields Market and bought something which would be essential in getting the job done. The shopkeeper gave me a very strange look as I tried to pay him for an orange ice lolly. After all, this was winter, and it was dark and cold outside.

I stepped out of the shop, unwrapped the lolly and pressed it against my throat. I wanted to numb the flesh on my neck in order to make it easier to cut. It's very hard to slash your own throat – the pain you experience half way through is enough to force you to stop, and I had to prevent this effect. After a minute or two, I could no longer feel my neck. Phase one of my plan was complete.

I walked over to my car purposefully, and got in. I unstrapped my knife, and put it on the seat next to me. I drove for a few minutes, found a side road, and turned in. It was time. In one fluid movement, I ran the blade from the base of my cheek to the top of my chest, and right through my throat. Blood spurted out all over me, and over the steering wheel. I watched it fly, and wondered how many seconds I had left on this earth.

A minute passed. Then another. Still I was bleeding, still I hadn't lost consciousness. This was frustrating. Dying was taking longer than I'd expected it to. I began to worry that it hadn't worked properly – that somehow I'd messed it up. Just in case, I decided to add a second level to the suicide, and started the engine.

As I drove deeper into London, I figured that any minute now I'd lose consciousness. When that happened, I'd lose control, and the car would crash. So if the wound didn't kill me, the accident would. I was absolutely serious this time. There was no way I wanted to walk away from this. I didn't care that in all probability, my death would now cause other casualties. I had lived a selfish life – it seemed only right to go out with a selfish death.

I put my foot down. I had to be sure. And yet as I accelerated, I realised something terrible: I was no longer bleeding. Blood had clotted around the wound much faster than it should have done. My overactive, coke-powered heart was saving my life! I cried out with utter despair, pulled over to the side of the road, and got out. I punched and kicked the car in utter rage. I had messed up everything in my life. Now I couldn't even manage to kill myself properly.

A few days after telling me that our marriage was finally over, I called Jacqui again. She hadn't changed her mind, and she was sure she never would, but she listened when I told her that I'd finally split up with Donna, and that I was feeling utterly depressed. And while she didn't want me back, that didn't mean that she didn't care.

'You need help, Arthur,' she told me.

'Yeah,' I agreed. 'But who is there who can help me?'

'You should see a counsellor. There's a man at my church who can help you.'

I managed to suppress my knee-jerk reaction to that statement. The last time she'd suggested that sort of thing, I'd gone ballistic and told her that I didn't want to speak to any 'bleedin' wet Christians'. This time, however, I knew that I needed to grow up a bit. I also knew that Jacqui was very friendly with these church people now, and I didn't want to offend her.

'I just want to get off the cocaine, off the gear, and come back to you.' I pleaded.

'No, Arthur,' she said sternly. 'This isn't about us. You've got to sort you out before we can ever talk about us.'

The fact that she even hinted that there might be a time when we could start to talk again about our relationship was the glimmer of hope that I needed. I agreed that I'd see this church bloke, even though I was certain that I'd hate him.

Jacqui gave me an address: Epping Forest Community Church. Just the name was enough to put me off – it sounded like the sort of place where people sat around painting rainbows and wearing socks with sandals. I gave it a go, though, and fulfilled my appointment with Vincent Wiffin, who was an 'elder', whatever that was supposed to mean. He was about sixty, and he was a big man, 6' 2", 16 stone, with a grey beard. He'd never have had any experience of anyone like me but he was a man's man, and certainly not what I expected. I'd always thought that church-going men were all weak, and that their faith was just a crutch for their weakness. This guy didn't look weak, to be fair to him.

I wasn't always vindictively opposed to the church. I used to go to weddings and christenings and say 'Hello' to the vicar, but that was as far as it ever went. It had been in more recent years, as Emma and then Jacqui had joined the church, that I'd become more tired of Christians. In the midst of our on-off period, Jacqui used to take me along to different functions, hoping that I'd hear a life-changing message and that something miraculous would happen. It never worked out like that though – at the first sign of evangelising I'd just lose my temper and storm out of there.

Now though, I knew that if I was going to get off the drugs and get my marriage back in order, I needed help. Jacqui seemed sure that this bloke was wise enough to be that person, and I was in no position to argue.

Vincent, or Vin as I called him, already knew a lot about me because Emma was in his congregation. She was also in the church youth group and, according to Vin, they were praying for me. I wasn't quite sure what I made of that.

I'm not sure why our meeting went the way it did. Maybe I wanted to shock Vin, or maybe I actually realised that it was time to talk to someone, it was probably a bit of both. I just poured it all out, and he just sat there gobsmacked, trying not to leave his mouth hanging open for too long at a time. I was telling him about the fights, the drugs, the sex and everything. He listened to every word, and to his credit, he never interrupted. That surprised me – I had expected him to hit me over the head with a Bible and pour out all his judgement on me. When I had finished, he thought for a few moments, and then simply said: 'Arthur, you've got to choose.'

'Eh?' That was a bit cryptic – I wasn't sure I understood.

'You need to choose what you're going to do with your life. You've got to choose between your wife and your mistress; between saving your family and starting another. You've got to choose between the life you've been living, and the life you say you want to live.'

When I walked out of there, my head was spinning. I knew what I wanted, but I also knew that it wasn't that easy. I wanted to choose a better life over the one that I was living, but I realised I wasn't strong enough to do it on my own. I agreed to meet Vin again, but still I was unsure whether he and his church really had much to say to me. I knew that whatever the outcome, Jacqui would think better of me if I kept meeting with him, and that alone was a good enough reason.

The next time we met, I went to his house. Even though I knew he was a church leader, I still went there tooled up. I had a knife strapped to my leg, and a knuckleduster in my pocket. If he bashed me with a Bible, I reasoned, then I could bash him back. We didn't fight though, and he really didn't try to quote his Bible at me – I told him more about my life, and he tried to hold back the grimaces as he listened, and listened. At the end of session, I felt a little better.

Vin spoke to Jacqui and suggested that next, it might be a good idea if he could meet the two of us together. But Jacqui wasn't interested. She assured him that our marriage really was over, whatever happened. Of course, I was devastated when he told me, but I couldn't possibly argue. It was a totally understandable decision from a woman who'd been cheated on, dragged through the dirt and then betrayed, time after time.

To his surprise, though, I asked if I could see him again. I was now finding our meetings therapeutic. I had never felt so listened to in all my life. And the third time I went to see him, I didn't even take weapons! Again, he let me dominate the conversation, again he just listened and listened. And again he repeated his advice: 'Arthur, the choice is yours.'

The following Sunday, I even went along to church. I was still high as a kite on coke and gear, and I made sure that I blended into the shadows at the back of the building, but I sat there, and I listened. I left quickly so that I wouldn't have to get stuck in boring conversation with any Christians, but the message stuck with me, or at least some of it did. 'Call out to God,' the preacher said that night. I wasn't entirely sure what that meant, but it stuck in my head.

I went straight over to the market, to do the Sunday-to-Monday shift at D.L. Bright. It was an eventful night and I had to do a fair bit of collecting. I ended up in more than one fight, and took a few lines of coke along the way in order to keep me sharp.

I returned to the market from my collection rounds with cuts on my fists and an ever-worsening pain in my chest. I was shattered and freezing cold – it was three in the morning. I leant up against the company van to gain a few seconds of rest, and as I did so, it struck me that this world I was inhabiting was madness, just total madness. I was supposed to be changing, and yet I was still right in the middle of this terrible, evil lifestyle.

Suddenly, it all seemed so simple. I couldn't live like this any more. And though there was bustle going on all around me with the Monday market, right then it felt like I was on my own. Something from the previous night's church service, or from one of my chats with Vin, re-entered my head, and I did something I never thought I'd do. I called out to God.

'God,' I said, not sure if this was the right step or if I was now losing the plot completely. 'If you're there, and you're the man they say you are, then you come and sort my life out.'

And then . . . nothing. There was no booming voice or opening of the heavens. The market went on around me, and I was still freezing. Everything was exactly the same. Well, almost.

One thing was different. I felt different. I felt calm, and peaceful, for the first time in years. I guess it was that moment of release, of handing my burdens, as they say in the recovery movement, over to a 'higher power'. And yet it was more than that – all of a sudden I found I had a new kind of mental strength. Right then, Vin's words came into my head again, and I knew that it was time to make my choice.

Instinctively, I knew what to do. I bent down and unstrapped the diver's knife from my left leg. I walked around to the back of D.L. Bright's, to where we had a great big skip which used to get filled up with rotten fruit and used packaging. I took the knife and hurled it into the skip. In this new life I was choosing, I would no longer be needing that.

The sense of peace didn't leave me. I went home to my mum's that morning, emptied out my toiletries bag, and filled it with every drug in my possession. There were powders, needles, spliffs, tablets and more – they filled the bag right to the brim. Then I took the bag, and put it in the hands of my mum, who was nearing seventy.

'Mum,' I said, aware that my mum was now in possession of enough drugs to earn her a long prison sentence, 'get rid of that lot. That's the cause of all my problems.'

They were practically the exact same words I'd said to Jacqui the very first time I'd gone back to her from Donna. But this time there was a big difference. This time, I really meant it. I wanted to be as far from those drugs as possible. They no longer held any attraction. They were part of my old life; now I'd chosen a new one.

When the drugs that were still in my system stopped taking effect, my long career of drug use came to an end. I never took so much as a line of coke again. My long-term addiction had completely disappeared – I simply chose to no longer take drugs. I wasn't sure how my heart would cope, but I decided it would just have to find a way. In my new life, there would be no place for drugs.

Neither would there be a place for violence. As I washed the blood off my hands, I also called my four-year stint as a violent hard man to an end. I knew that I could no longer act that way.

My old life was over, but just as that chaplain had suggested, there had indeed been more than one way out of it. Now I could begin to think about a new life. But the one thing I wanted more than anything seemed completely unattainable. Jacqui wasn't even prepared to consider taking me back. Peaceful and calm but uncertain about the future, I wondered what this new life might entail.

12

Resurrection

I had asked God to take control of my life. I didn't have any great theological understanding of what that meant. All I knew was that I couldn't go on living the way I had been, and I couldn't change on my own. For a man who had always wanted to believe that he was in control, this was a big step.

All I had done was call out to God. I hadn't got down on my knees and prayed some clever prayer. I hadn't worked my way through some kind of ten-week course at church. I'd just told God, that if he was out there somewhere, I wanted him to come and sort me out.

After I'd disposed of my drug stash, I called Vin and told him what had happened. He was delighted to hear about it, and told me that I had made the right decision. He wasn't at all surprised to hear about the strange feeling of peace and calm that I'd experienced, or that I'd managed to seemingly put a decade of drug use behind me.

'That sounds like God, Arthur,' he said.

I told him that I was keen to find out more. He invited me to come to see him again, but this time, we would actually look at the Bible. Just a few weeks earlier, that kind of suggestion might have led me to laugh in his face or even hit him. Not now. Now I was thirsty to know more about God, and how it was possible to know him like a bloke knew his best mate. I couldn't yet get my head around the fact that God, who presumably created the universe, could also be prepared to get his hands dirty with a washed-up old loser like me. How did he have the time to intervene in my drug addiction, or to give me a nice warm feeling? Surely he had more important places to be, like down the church with the blokes in the socks and sandals?

After I got off the phone with Vin, I went straight round to Jacqui's house, to tell her the same story. Because she'd been hanging around at the church, I'd assumed that this was exactly what she wanted.

'I think I've become a Christian, Jacqui,' I announced proudly as the door opened.

She nearly slammed it again in my face. She was totally unimpressed.

'As far as I'm concerned, Arthur, you ain't.'

My face fell. She let me into the house, but she wasn't prepared to discuss the idea that I'd somehow found God. She was sure that this would just be another one of my lies, another strategy in my constant attempts to weave my way back into her good books. She wasn't a Christian herself, although I'd assumed that she must have been. She'd been going along to the church for company, and because Emma and James were now both involved in the youth groups. But she hadn't 'found God'.

Emma had, of course, and when she saw me, she immediately noticed something different. Up to that point, Emma had been very, very stern with me, but as a Christian, she prayed for me every night. She prayed that God would somehow intervene in my life, before it careered off the rails entirely and ended in death. She prayed that her mum and dad might somehow have a strong and secure marriage again. Now, when she saw me for the first time after I'd called out to God, she was instantly convinced that something had changed. She tried to persuade Jacqui, too.

'Mum, I think he's telling the truth.'

'No, Emma,' Jacqui replied, trying not to get too upset. 'It's just another lie.'

I said nothing. I was stunned by the irony of the situation. The first time in years that I'd told Jacqui the truth, and she told me I was lying!

Jacqui left Emma and me alone in the kitchen, and for the first time in far too long, my little girl flung her arms around me and kissed me. I knew that she believed me, and it was enough to keep me going. Over the weeks that followed, Emma became a rock to me – she was like a counsellor. She was still desperate to see me get back with her mum, but she was also wise about the situation. She advised me to back off for a little while, and let Jacqui observe the changes in my life from a safe distance.

I continued to see Vin every week, but now instead of it being about him listening to my long grisly stories, it was about friendship. Vin offered a totally new kind of friendship to the ones I was used to.

One of my best 'friends' was Billy Dando, the gun enthusiast. He used to get steroids for me, and so he was influential in getting me into serious drug use. He wasn't a very nice man. On one of the occasions when Jacqui and I split up, she went to see Billy to see if he knew where I was. He could see that she was upset, so he asked her if she wanted him to break my kneecaps if he found me. And this was someone who was meant to be my mate!

So since that was my benchmark for friendship, it's hardly surprising that this church leader treated me slightly better. When we met, I could ask any question about God and faith. Since I'd grown up in a Christian country, I'd always referred to myself as a 'Christian', but talking to Vin I realised that there was so much more to it than I had ever understood. Week by week we took things a few steps further. He explained that prayer was nothing to worry about – that you didn't have to have some sort of clever form of poetic words that you read out, but that you could just say what you were feeling to God, as if he was a bloke sitting next to you. I tried that, sitting there with Vin, and it felt strangely normal.

Usually my prayers were quite simple: I'd say thanks to God for helping me to give up the gear and the coke, and then I'd ask him to help me out with a few more things. Every time we prayed, I asked God to bring Jacqui back to me, and although that prayer didn't seem to get answered, others did. I was still terrified about the pains in my chest, and so I asked God if he could somehow get rid of them. I knew that Jesus had healed the sick and Vin reckoned he still did it now. Well, remembering that X-ray, I was one sick man. So I prayed to God simply, asking him if he'd heal my heart.

Within minutes, the pain in my chest had disappeared. I wasn't sure if somehow this was my mind playing tricks on me, but it no longer hurt. Having had the pain for so long, I had begun to get used to it. It was background pain, a constant dull ache and a reminder of the time bomb in my chest. But now it had gone. I told Vin, and although he was ecstatic, again he wasn't surprised. I began to realise that I was messing with some very serious power here. I was stronger than most men on this earth, but I couldn't do things like this. It seems strange to say it, but God really impressed me.

The pain never came back. From that point on, I could never deny that God was real. A few weeks earlier, I'd stood at the gates of death, with an addiction I couldn't handle and a serious heart condition. Now they'd both disappeared, and all I'd done was pray a couple of times.

It was mind-blowing. Suddenly, my head was full of questions. In an attempt to answer them, Vin suggested that we start to look at the Bible together. So from then on when we met, we'd read these Bible passages and talk about them. Mainly, we read about Jesus, this bloke from 2,000 years ago who I'd previously thought of as a sweet little baby who grew into a mild-mannered wimp. When I actually came to read about his life, however, I realised that my perceptions had been wrong. For instance, this guy had been a carpenter. Now most people probably overlook this as a side detail, but since I was also

a carpenter by trade, that told me quite a lot. He'd
have spent his career carrying heavy lumps of wood
about and working with his hands. He couldn't
have done this job without being a strong man, a
muscular man – all carpenters have to be because of
the weight of the wood they work with. So my picture of Jesus wasn't of some skinny little bloke with
a straggly beard, it was of someone like me.

As I read and discussed the words with Vin, it all
seemed to make sense. The Christian faith was like
the good news that no one had ever bothered to tell
me about life. And central to it was something I'd
always assumed was beyond me: forgiveness.

The core of the whole Christian message is the
idea that any person, however low they've sunk,
whatever they've done in their lives, can receive
ultimate forgiveness. It's possible for any man – a
gangster, a murderer, anyone – to turn his back on
his old way of living, and receive forgiveness from
God. It is hard to put into words how choked I felt
when I realised that as far as God was concerned, all
the rotten, dirty, terrible things I'd done in my life
were now in the past. My drugs, my affair, my violence – all of it was forgiven and dealt with by God.

That didn't mean, as Vin pointed out, that the
consequences of those actions could now be easily
dismissed or forgotten. And just because God had

forgiven me, it didn't follow that Jacqui would be able to – or even want to.

It was then that I realised that simply praying for God to bring Jacqui back to me was the wrong thing to be doing. All this was in God's hands now, and it was possible that in his view, the best thing for Jacqui would be to stay away from me. So for the first time, I prayed a different prayer: 'Lord, please let Jacqui be happy, and if it's your will, please bring us back together.'

As I said 'Amen' to that prayer, I knew that my future was uncertain. But I also knew that my desire to grow and continue in the Christian faith was no longer linked to trying to get Jacqui back. I had turned my life over to God now for good.

I kept working down at the market for about six months after my conversion. I'd cut out all the villainy, yet I was still involved in credit control and trying to retrieve Doug Bright's debts. Now though, I knew I couldn't use my fists. My Bible studies with Vin showed me that this wasn't a Christian way to live, or to settle disagreements. God, my example, is 'slow to anger', so now I had to try to be that way, too.

It didn't become any less tough down there, though. It was still a mean place to work, full of dodgy deals and shady characters. I was still being offered coke on a regular basis, and I have to admit that while I didn't take any, I was often tempted to. I was also drawing strange looks from many of my colleagues when I kept turning down stolen goods and illegal moneymaking opportunities.

The funny thing, however, was that I actually brought in more money collecting debts as a Christian than I ever had as a faithless thug. This was because word had got round that I had 'gone religious', and people thought that I must have gone mad. Whenever I saw them now, I had a smile on my face, and tried to tell them about Jesus. They couldn't get their chequebooks out fast enough! They thought that the coke had finally got to me and turned me into some kind of Bible-quoting nut-case, and that apparently frightened them even more than the old me.

After a while though, I knew I could no longer work in that environment. The enemies I'd made over several years weren't quite as forgiving as God, and they didn't care if I'd apparently turned over a new leaf. There were still plenty of men who had a beef with me, and even those who wanted me dead. Now I was a Christian, I knew I couldn't fight fire with fire, and if I got fronted by one of these blokes I was going to be in trouble – I'd have to just take a beating, or worse. Eventually, after one such confrontation, I decided to walk away from the market for good. Doug Bright shook my hand, and wished me all the best. Though I'd once thought it impossible, I was stepping away from my career of violence, and starting again.

Despite Vin's best efforts to get Jacqui and me talking, she still wasn't interested in any reconciliation. She made it clear that she didn't want me at her church either, because that was her space. So I started to go to any old church I could find.

But God was working in Jacqui's life, too, and at a similar time to me she also made the decision to become a Christian. For her, it was a slightly different calculation, not based so much on forgiveness. The defining issue in Jacqui's life – thanks to me – was brokenness, and she realised that she could no longer cope alone. So one Sunday morning, in the early hours, she asked God to step into her life and be her comforter. He did exactly as she asked, but that didn't suddenly turn her into a mug. She was still badly hurt by what I had done and couldn't be expected to instantly forgive me for the years of abuse I'd dealt her.

After a few months, Jacqui finally made a concession to me. She could see from my uncharacteristic staying power that I was serious about this Christianity business, and so she agreed that I could come to church with her and the kids. There was an important rule though: I had to sit on the other side of the church. I respected and obeyed her request, and it wasn't long before she then allowed me to sit with her.

It was strange at first joining their congregation. I wasn't a fool – I knew that they'd helped Jacqui and Emma through the hell I'd subjected them to – and so I knew that many of the people sitting around me would know who I was and what I'd done. Even though I felt slightly awkward though, I also felt that it was incredibly important that we were in the same church if we were ever going to make a go of things again in the future.

During one of our meetings, Vin brought up the subject of baptism. In the Christian faith, the practice of adult baptism usually means that they dunk people in big pools of water – a little bit like diving into a swimming pool with your clothes on. Had you told me about it a few months earlier, I would have told you that you were barking, but now I understood the spiritual significance, and it made sense to me. Baptism is about making a public declaration of faith – that's why they do it in the middle of a church service with hundreds of people watching. There's also a deeper significance though: the waters symbolise the change from the old way of living to a new one. When you rise out of the waters, you're effectively saying, 'I've been born again.' As soon as Vin explained all this, I knew that it was something I had to do.

Emma had already been through this process when I'd been off on one of my many trips. Jacqui and James were also keen to do it, and so the three of us got baptised together. And right after that, I became convinced that Jacqui and I were going to get back together. I don't know why – I was just so sure.

Being a Christian, I couldn't really continue taking part in my old hobbies. That meant that I was often at a loose end so I found something to focus my mind: I decided to make a model boat for my mum – a wooden galleon. I was engrossed in this process one day, sitting in my mum's kitchen, when the phone rang. It was Jacqui. I had been following Emma's advice and backing off, which meant I rarely called her. So I was very excited when she finally picked up the phone to call me.

'Arthur,' she said softly. 'I think it's time we had a chat.'

'OK . . .' I replied, unsure. Obviously I didn't know what this meant. It was possible that she wanted to talk through getting a divorce.

'Why don't you come over this evening?'

I didn't need any encouragement. In a flash I downed my tools, jumped in the shower, and covered myself from head to toe in the best aftershave I could lay my hands on. I literally sprinted the short distance to Jacqui's house.

Jacqui opened the door with half a smile, and I knew instantly that it wasn't bad news. She looked even more beautiful, standing there, than she did on the day I married her, and feelings rushed through my body that I hadn't experienced since I was a teenager. I was so desperate to get her back, and to pull our wonderful little family – which I had done my best to completely ruin – back together for good.

She showed me in, and we sat down to talk. We didn't get up again until 3 o'clock in the morning. We talked about everything – Donna, God, the market, our kids, our past – anything and everything came up, and we had the best and fullest conversation we'd had in ten years. We laughed together, we reminisced, and she filled me with hope for the future – so much so that I slightly embarrassed myself at the end of the evening.

'Well Jacq,' I said, 'I'd better be going . . . although . . . I could stay here tonight . . .'

She smirked at me. 'You must be joking,' she scoffed.

My face fell, and I realised I'd moved much too fast. 'Sorry Jacq, I didn't mean to . . .'

'But if you're lucky,' she interrupted, 'then maybe one day.'

I left there walking on air. I got a peck on the cheek from my wife as I left, and it was as if we'd had three hours of passionate sex. At last, there seemed to be a light at the end of the tunnel.

After our conversation, Jacqui agreed at last that we should meet together with Vin once a week to talk about our marriage. I guess you could call it marriage reconciliation, but it didn't have that official title. All we'd do is go to his house and together talk through the last ten years, being as honest as we could, and with a view to one day getting things back on track. Sitting there listening to Jacqui describe all the things I'd put her through – and particularly the loneliness of being an abandoned parent – was one of the hardest things I've ever had to sit and take. I was so ashamed of myself, and angry with the person that I used to be. I couldn't believe that I'd let myself get away with so much –

it was like my conscience had evaporated for those years.

Being a man, I had hoped for a quick fix – that after a couple of weeks of classes, Jacqui would simply come running back into my arms, with everything forgiven. But it wasn't as simple as that – having been left seven times, Jacqui was still a bit wary of trusting me completely. The one thing that was needed, according to Vin, was time – for Jacqui to heal and me to prove myself. That didn't mean that our relationship didn't continue to drift back together, it just meant that a quick fix was out of the question. We started dating all over again, just like we had thirty years or so earlier, and we'd go out for a nice meal in the evening and talk until late. But at the end of every date, despite what I always hoped for, I'd take her home, and then go back to my mum's, alone.

One night, Jacqui finally put a time frame on things, and suggested that at the end of the year, maybe we could get back together. It was only May, though, and by now I was getting frustrated in all sorts of ways, physically as well as mentally. A man of my age could only cope with living with his elderly mother for so long, much as I loved her. Jacqui had made a decision though, and I had to respect it. If I could prove my worth, I knew that eventually I'd have my family back.

Every single time that my marriage had looked like it was back on track over those tempestuous five years, the same spectre had appeared on the horizon: Donna. Once again, at this critical moment, she made another appearance. This time, however, things would be different.

I was having a cup of coffee at Jacqui's house when her phone rang. It was Donna: she couldn't find me anywhere else, and needed to talk to me. She wanted to know whether there was any chance that we'd ever get back together. With Jacqui standing by my side, desperate to know what was being said, I gave the only answer that was in my head. 'I'm sorry Donna. It's never going to happen.'

She was upset, but had expected me to say that. In which case, she wanted to move out of the flat, and back to Wales. She asked if she could rent out the flat so that she could still pay the mortgage, and I agreed.

As I put the phone down on Donna, I realised that there was something that I hadn't told Jacqui. It was a confession with the potential to make her so angry that it threw our reconciliation right out of the window, but I knew I had to tell her. Slowly, I began to tell Jacqui everything about the little love nest that I'd bought with Donna, completely without her knowledge. And then – the sting in the tail – that I had forged her signature to get it. This news might have knocked some people off balance, but not Jacqui. Having already forgiven me for so much, she took this piece of information in her stride. What mattered to her was that I'd never again be alone with Donna, and I swore that I wouldn't be.

But a few weeks later, Donna rang me again, and told me the truth. She couldn't find anyone to rent the flat, and she hadn't paid the mortgage herself for several months. She was being taken to court, and because my name (and Jacqui's) was on the mortgage, I might need to go, too. Again, I knew that the best policy would be to tell Jacqui everything, and again she exceeded my expectations. Knowing that I would have to go and meet with Donna to talk the issue through, Jacqui offered to come with me. She was so committed now to getting our relationship back together, and clearing the decks of the past, that she was prepared to sit across a table from her, from 'the other woman' who was partly to blame for the hell she'd been through.

'If you can't say it in front of me, you shouldn't be saying it to her,' she told me.

I was so pleased that Jacqui was prepared to support me in this way. Considering the history, I can only conclude that it was God, and the change he had made in my heart, that meant that I was no longer in the least bit tempted by Donna. And that was genuinely the case – I no longer had eyes for any woman in the world besides my wife. I guess you could say that God healed me of my lust problem.

Donna admitted that she had no way of paying the mortgage and Jacqui suggested that we simply took it over from her, absorbing the financial problem. The flat would only belong to us, and we'd be free to rent it out in order to earn some money. Donna reluctantly agreed, and promised to send the paperwork through.

She didn't, though. She went back to Wales and left the whole situation unresolved. I never heard from her again.

Having 'dated' me over a period of months, Jacqui could see a definite change in me, the kind of which she knew I couldn't fake. Our body language was getting closer and closer, and we started to do much more together as a couple. Vin suggested that we could take part in a short marriage skills course which the church was running. We went along and enjoyed ourselves – I found that there was a lot of wisdom to be found in the Bible about how to conduct your relationships.

At the end of the course, Vin asked if we would be prepared to stand up at the front of our church and do something to demonstrate how reconciliation can work, even in the most desperate and unlikely circumstances. He asked us if we'd be prepared to renew our wedding vows.

I was all for the idea of course, but I didn't expect the same reaction from Jacqui, who'd been talking about getting back together at the end of the year. To my surprise, however, she agreed. A date was set – 1 August 1993. It was twenty-two years and one day exactly from the day we got married – 31 July 1971.

We had the renewal service, but as far as I was concerned we got married again. That night, I'm proud to say, I moved back in with Jacqui and we made love again for the first time in a very long while. In October, we even managed to get a bit of money together, with the help of a few friends and had a second honeymoon.

At last, my shattered life had truly been fitted back together. What had seemed totally impossible at the start of the year, by the grace of God was made possible. My wife welcomed me back as her husband, and my equally gracious children welcomed me back as a father, a job I was determined to do much better. From the brink of destruction, I had clawed my way back, and I hadn't done it on my own.

13

Restoration

It was fantastic to be living together as a family again, although it wasn't always easy. They'd forgiven me, but I knew it would still take a long time for Jacqui, especially, to truly begin to forget what had happened. We talked a lot, sometimes all of us together, more often just Jacqui and me. We went over everything that had happened to us, good and bad, through the twenty-five years and more that we'd been together. The fact that we were still sitting at the same breakfast table now seemed like ultimate proof not only of the existence of God, but also of the fact that we were always meant to be together.

We went over the last, most difficult period, when we'd both been alone and at the very end of our wits. Jacqui was crying herself to sleep in one part of Essex, while I had been contemplating suicide in another. On the early hours of one Sunday morning in March 1993, Jacqui told me that she had called out to God, and asked him to be her comforter. As she told me this, I became intrigued. I'd never heard her mention this exact time before, and so I asked her if she could be any more precise about the date. She replied that it was the second Sunday of the month. I was astonished. On the second Sunday of March 1993, early in the morning, freezing in the car park of Spitalfields Market, I too had called out to God. In completely separate areas, having not spoken in days, my estranged wife and I had both sought God at pretty much exactly the same moment.

It was just another confirmation that God had been part of the picture all along. In my mind, there is just no way that this happened coincidentally.

God also involved himself in our lives in some very physical ways. I would find that if I prayed something to God, more often than not, something would happen. One of my biggest concerns was my heart, the X-rays of which had terrified me. There were stretch marks shown to be present, and I had been warned by a doctor that giving up drugs could in fact kill me. That was exactly what I had done after becoming a Christian, at which point the pain in my chest had disappeared. Still, I was worried that the problem might still be there. I thought that this might be a thing to pray about, and so very simply, I asked God to heal my heart.

A few years later, I had to go into hospital for a small hernia operation, not a major thing. When they were doing various checks, they looked through my records and saw that I had a history of serious heart damage. The doctor was also extremely concerned because according to their weight/height charts, I was seriously obese – weighing in at over seventeen stone. Of course, the majority of this was muscle, and when she examined me, she agreed that I was probably an exception to the chart.

The examination also surprised her, however. She had to conclude that I was in extremely good shape – in fact, she could find no evidence of the heart problem. Nothing whatsoever – no stretch marks, no swelling. I told her that an awful lot of people had prayed for me, and that I believed that God had cured me. She just smiled and went ahead with the operation.

Within a few months, my marriage was as good as it had ever been. We were having fun again, really enjoying one another's company, and spending a far better quality of time together. I couldn't remember a time when things had been better between us – in every department. My relationship with Emma and James was completely restored too – somehow both of them were able to find the grace and the strength of character to forgive and accept me.

James had grown into a fine young man, thanks almost in total to the input of his devoted mother. I hadn't really been around to have a real relationship with him, but I was determined to make up for lost time now. As I got to know him all over again, I was both sad at the thought of what I'd missed out on, but immensely proud to call him my son. I was equally proud of Emma, a girl who was able to see the world for what it was far earlier than I ever did.

Our family was stronger than ever, and this time, the foundations that it was built upon were rock solid. That's not to say there weren't bumps in the road, but when they came along, we found ourselves well equipped to deal with them.

For example, a few years later, I got a letter from the building society through which I'd bought the flat with Donna. The letter explained that due to non-payment from Donna, who had never come back to us on our offer to assume control of the property, they had foreclosed the mortgage and sold the flat off. They do this in an auction, and often fail to make much or any profit as a result. In fact sometimes, such as in this instance, there is actually a shortfall, which they still expect to be covered. The shortfall on the flat was £4,893, and since they couldn't find Donna, and I didn't know where she was, they wanted it from me.

I was philosophical about it. I thought I could probably just add the amount to our mortgage, and have to pay a few extra pounds a month for the next ten or fifteen years. But then I read the letter again. My jaw almost dropped to the floor. I'd misread a speck of dust as a decimal point, the shortfall was actually £48,930, nearly fifty grand. I was devastated, as was Jacqui. We had no way of getting this kind of money, and I knew that this could lead to bankruptcy and losing our house. Four years after our reconciliation, it felt as if the past had finally caught up with me after all.

Desperate, I went to see a friend of mine who was a solicitor and told him about it. He suggested there might be some clever ways out of having to face the debt, but I didn't want to do that. I told him that I wanted to do it right, even if that meant losing everything again. He shook his head at me like I was an idiot, and said he'd talk to the Building Society and explain my situation. He didn't hold out too much hope though; I was probably heading for a big fall. As I left his office, I said a short prayer: 'God, I know this is my fault, and I deserve to receive the consequences of my actions, but if there's any way you can help . . .'

As promised, my solicitor spoke to the building society, and then waited for a reply. It came a few weeks later, and knocked all of us off our feet. Their letter said that if I paid immediately, they would accept £5,000 as a full and final settlement. I couldn't write the cheque out quickly enough.

I'm sure that God was heavily involved in the resolution of that problem. It could have ruined us, and I honestly don't believe any solicitor is capable of shaving 90 per cent off a bank charge. I believe that because I approached the issue in the way that God would have wanted me to – insisting that we play it fair and do what was right – that he did the rest. Although it's important to remember that I didn't simply get the bill written off – I still had to find five grand, which was a very significant sum of money to me.

Even though I had started a new kind of life then, the things that I had done in my old life still had consequences that would sometimes impact the present. My reputation as a hard and dangerous man didn't just evaporate – in fact, now that I'd started talking about religion, they thought I'd gone mad and become even more dangerous! There were men in the East End of London who would have happily taken my life at one stage; I guess that over time they realised that I was no longer a threat to them and decided not to pursue me. But the game I had been playing over those years at the market was a game of death. There are certain people who only know one way out of a situation, and that is murder. If you front up to these men, there's only one way that they understand. They're mad.

I'd had plenty of these encounters in my debt collecting days, and I somehow managed to survive. I guess I learned when to fight and when to walk away. I didn't expect, however, to have to make a similar decision several years after my conversion.

We put our house in Loughton up for sale, and one day while I was out, a couple came around to look at it. James showed them around, and must have done a very good job – they agreed to buy. They rang me later to talk about the price, and although I'd never seen this guy face to face, the sale was agreed. However, circumstances changed, and we were suddenly no longer ready to move, so I had to call this bloke back and tell him that I'd decided I didn't want to sell it after all. I said that I was sorry, but I'd reconsidered what I was doing.

'You can't do this!' he shouted, 'I've paid money for a survey.'

'I'm sorry about that,' I replied. 'I'll happily give you the money for that.'

That placated him, but then his girlfriend came on to the phone.

'You can't pull out!' she screamed. 'This is our dream home. We've fallen in love with it. You can't just pull out for no reason. It's outrageous.' She possibly used more choice language than this, but I'll choose not to remember it.

'I'm very sorry,' I said. 'Things have changed. We're not ready to move.'

'Well, we'll just wait until you are. When can you move?'

'I'm sorry, I'm not going to sell it to you. Now I've apologised, and agreed to compensate you. I don't need to talk to you any more, and I'd appreciate it if you don't call me again.' I hung up the phone. I wrote a cheque, sent it to the estate agent, and thought no more of it.

A few months later, we did sell the house, to a different buyer. We'd exchanged contracts, and we were only a couple of weeks from our moving date. Jacqui and I went out shopping one day, and while we were out, James was working on his car on our driveway. A BMW pulled up outside the house, and this typical Essex loudmouth, in his early thirties, gets out. James recognised him as the bloke who first agreed to buy the house.

He launched into a verbal assault on James, and went absolutely ballistic. 'You can tell your old man I know who he is,' he screamed. 'He thinks he's a hard nut, but I know everything about him. He's dead, he's nothing. He might have been a face in his time but not any more – I'm going to kill him.'

James didn't confront him, and just backed off – clearly he has more sense in these situations than his father. The bloke left and went to the estate agents to put on a similar routine there. When I got home James told me what had happened. I was furious. Though I was a Christian, I was still human, and I couldn't take the thought that my son had been shouted at and threatened like this. It was nothing to do with him.

I don't know how this guy knew about my past. He was twenty years younger than me, and it's very unlikely that I'd have ever had an encounter with him, unless I threw him out of the country club as a lad, possibly. It's more likely that I had a brush with his dad, whoever his dad might have been. But he knew who I was, and who I had been, and I didn't like it.

That night, I suffered a small relapse of my old ways. Infuriated by this bloke, I drove around to his house (I had his address from when we'd agreed to sell the house) and decided that I'd have a go at him. I sat outside his house, not really sure how I'd got there, and wondered how this might play out. As I saw it, there were two options – either he'd lose his bottle and turn away from me, or we would have a fight.

He might have been twenty years younger than me, but I was still in very good shape, and a power-lifting champion again so it could be that if I'd fought him, I'd win. But if I had bashed him, I knew that this was not the sort of bloke who would know when to stop. He was nutty enough to come after me and my family. He'd threaten my son, he'd vandalise my property, and he'd keep going, because people like that don't know how to stop until either you're dead on the floor or they are.

Sitting in the car outside his house, and thinking all this through, I had a moment of clarity. This wasn't who I was any more. That 'turning the other cheek' business isn't just a catchphrase – it's good sense. Driving away from that house without ever getting out of my car was probably the best decision I made that year.

As a Christian, I continued to compete in power-lifting competitions around the world. Of course, I was now lifting drug free and at first that made things more difficult. But I continued to train, and continued to grow stronger. In 1996, my persever-ance was rewarded as I won both the British and European titles in the unrecognised powerlifting organisation. I would have gone on to enter the World Championship that year, but years of abusing my body had begun to catch up with me. I began to experience excruciating pain in my knees, and entered a long period of treatment, surgery and subsequent recovery.

In 1996, I had serious surgery on my right leg and two years later the focus was switched to the left leg. In all, I had six operations: one minor, one major and one 'major plus' operation on each.

What had happened was that over the years my legs had literally collapsed on the inside, meaning that I had become very bow legged. By 1996, the pain caused by this had become so bad that I couldn't walk. I went to see my doctor but he told me that he couldn't do anything to help. I was in a lot of pain, and so as a Christian I asked a lot of people to pray for me. One of the women in our church ran a physiotherapist business – in fact she was Rod Stewart's physio. She told me that she knew an expert who was very good with knees: a surgeon who I should go to visit. So I got an appointment to see this surgeon at Wellington Hospital, in St John's Wood, London.

His response was very different. He told me that they could definitely operate and actually straighten my legs.

'OK!' I exclaimed, relieved. 'How much will it cost?'

'About £8,000,' he replied, straight-faced. 'For each leg.'

'Sixteen grand! But I can't afford that.'

'I'm sorry – they're not my fees. They're the hospital's.'

I was desperate. 'Can't you do it at another hospital?' I asked. At the time, Jacqui was working at another hospital, and they said that they could do the operation at a discount for me.

'I'm sorry,' he replied, 'but I'm contracted to only work here.'

I was devastated. The pain was getting worse even as I was talking to him.

'Although,' he said, thinking, 'I do know another man, who is capable of doing this operation.'

My heart filled with hope as he handed me the details of this other surgeon, a Mr Ireland. And I became even more elated when first Mr Ireland agreed to do the operation, and then the hospital agreed to house it for just £4,000 per leg.

I had a minor operation first, where he did the investigation work. Then came the main operation, called 'major plus' surgery. A major plus operation means it is in the league of major heart surgery. It is bigger than a knee replacement because of the anaesthetic, the reconstruction and the time in plaster. He had to cut the leg in half under the knee, and take it apart, cutting through the bone. Because the leg had literally bowed, he took a wedge out of the bottom bone and a wedge out of the top piece, the piece just under the kneecap. He then put the two together, and this literally straightened me up. Then he pinned it on either side, broke the joint and broke the kneecap, and then straightened the leg. I was in plaster from my toe to my hip for three months. I only had the one leg done at a time because Mr Ireland said that I wouldn't be able to stand the pain from both. I had another major operation three months later, just to remove the pins.

Once I was walking again, I obviously did so with a huge limp – I had one straight leg and one that was bowed. So in 1998, I returned to see Mr Ireland and went through the same long and painful process. Once I finally recovered, I felt like a new man, and in one way at least, I wasn't quite the man I'd been before. When I'd gone in for my first operation, I'd stood 6' ½" tall. After surgery, I was 5' 10". I'd lost two and a half inches in height!

I waited for a number of years, and decided eventually that I would return to my sport. Yet although I'd received a lifetime ban for competing in South Africa, I felt it was worth giving the recognised powerlifting federation, the British Amateur Weightlifting Association (or BAWLA), a call before I entered any competitions. After all, I was now a very different man to the one that they'd thrown out over a decade earlier.

I contacted Wally Holland, the president of BAWLA, who I knew, and explained some of my story to him. I asked him if there was any chance that they'd consider reinstating me. He said that as far as he was concerned, it sounded like the right thing to do, but the decision wasn't his – I had to talk to the BAWLA secretary John Lear. John was also an old friend, and had been my teacher when I became a coach. He was a very intelligent man and a university lecturer. When we spoke, he told me that he had just read an article about me and my story, in *The Times*. They had interviewed me, as many journalists had when they'd heard about the change in my life.

I explained things to John and told him that I was keen to get my BAWLA certificate back if it was in any way possible. I mentioned that I'd spoken to Wally and that he was happy with me getting reinstated as long as John, as the head of coaching, approved.

The Times article seemed to work in my favour. Though he wasn't a Christian, John thought my story was tremendous, and agreed that the association should make an exception on my part. I was over-joyed – yet another part of my fractured life had been completely restored. From that day on, I only lifted in official competitions.

The standard was high, but with my freshly-repaired legs I felt better than ever. I won the world title in 2002, and another – my fourth – in 2005.

Winning those world titles – along with a number of additional British and European tournaments – seemed to me to be the final chapter in my restoration. From a position where I had nothing, every-thing had been given back to me. My marriage was completely healed, and remains as solid as it has ever been. I enjoy a fantastic relationship with my children, and now my beautiful granddaughter, after Emma gave birth to Kate in 2005. I have a home, a car, and enough money to get by. My heart has been completely healed, my drug addictions have completely disappeared, and I am a British, European and World Champion, in the officially recognised arm of the sport.

Looking back at my life, there is no other way to explain what happened – a total and unequivocal change in my lifestyle, circumstances, health and happiness – apart from the hand of God.

He lifted me out of the pit, and set my feet on a rock. I have never looked back, and I never will.

Ten Years Later . . .

I stood shivering in the frozen Russian prison, determined to put up a good show against my colossal opponent. He snorted at me, like a bull, his breath streaming out of his nostrils. It was his turn first, and all I could do was sit back and watch.

Two guards struggled into the centre of the room, carrying a bar, and rolling various heavy weights. They assembled the bar at a fairly attainable weight, and my opponent lifted it with ease. He smiled at me, threw down the bar, and motioned for me to do the same.

By now, with four world, six European, and nine British powerlifting titles under my belt, I knew two things. One, I could lift considerably more than this fella, however big he might be, and two, you have to play the crowd. I stood over the bar, crouched, and pretended to really exert myself in lifting it to my knees. In fact, I was barely breaking a sweat (a shame considering the temperature), but the Russian prisoners didn't know that.

Eventually, I dropped the bar and stepped back. More weight was added, and again, my opponent lifted, although with a little less sureness this time around. Again, I faked a battle with the bar, finally succeeding, to the roar of the crowd. A third time their man lifted, and a third time I responded in kind.

Finally, even more weights were added. My opponent did not look at all certain that he could lift this bar, it seemed to be above his personal best. He grabbed hold of it, got it to about an inch from the ground, and then turned purple. The weights crashed to the ground, drawing gasps from all around the balcony. If I could lift this, I would be the winner.

I wasn't here as a prisoner. It would mark a pretty serious decline from 1993 if I had been. In fact, I was in Russia in a kind of ambassadorial role for the Christian faith. It was something I had done more and more ever since I'd got my life back on track. Sometimes I would travel with other powerlifting Christians; at other times I would go out on my own. I would lift weights and tell stories of how my life had been saved and radically changed by God. This was one of those trips, but before I could tell them my story, I had to earn their respect.

I stood behind the bar, and looked at it long and hard. This was my moment to play the crowd. I knew that this kind of lift was well within my comfort zone, and to this point I had been trying hard to convince the prisoners that it was not. Now, as I reached down to pick up the weights, I relaxed my body, and took hold. Almost effortlessly, I plucked the bar from the ground, and raised it in a perfect dead lift. I allowed a broad smile to escape, and the crowd roared. Stunned by this feat of strength, my opponent gave me a warm handshake. I had won everyone over – him included.

So, after I had proved my mettle, the prisoners were happy to sit and listen to what I had to say. Through a translator, I began to tell them the story of my life.

'My name is Arthur White, and I've come all the way from London, England to speak to you today. I'm the current and nine-times British Powerlifting champion. I've been European Champion six times, and four times Champion of the World. I've been in the Guinness Book of Records between 1982 and 1999. I've broken somewhere in the region of fifty or sixty British, European and world records, a number of which I still hold. But let me tell you something – I'd sacrifice everything I've ever won, to know Jesus Christ. A decade ago he stretched his hand out and he dragged me out of the pit. He stood me on the rock, which is his Word, and he set me free.

'Powerlifting was my God – this is what I worshipped. My whole life revolved around powerlifting. When I arrived on my honeymoon after getting married, the first thing I did was find the nearest gym. But my obsession had a high price, and I ended up getting involved in the taking of anabolic steroids and cocaine. For between eight and ten years, I was a drug addict – hooked. As a direct result of that addiction, I lost everything that ever meant anything to me. In four years, I blew something like £150,000 in cash on my cocaine addiction – now that's a lot of money. I had an adulterous affair with a young woman – I left my wife and lost my children. I lost my homes, my business, my jobs, my cars, my money – and somehow I still thought I was in control of my life.

'Taking steroids and cocaine was what ruled and was ruining my life. Nine of my good friends – all bodybuilders and powerlifters – all died through steroid and cocaine addictions. I thought I was in control of my life, and yet my life was out of control. Everybody else was doing it, so that's what I did. You choose your friends wrong; you choose to run with the wrong crowd, and believe me you'll be dragged down.

'Due to the drugs, my heart ballooned to the size of a small football – it was going to explode. I attempted suicide on a number of occasions. There were men in the East End of London who wanted to take my life. My life ten years ago was over. There was only one way for me to go ten years ago, and that was down, and that was death. My life was finished. Everything that meant anything to me, I lost. And yet I still thought I was in control of my life. There are consequences for your actions: if you choose wisely you'll have a glorious life. If you choose wrongly, then you'll just end up dead.

'Ten years ago, my life was almost at an end. I was running an illegal debt collecting business in the East End of London. I used to carry with me a twelve-inch diver's knife strapped to my forearm, and I would draw and use that knife as I needed. I remember stabbing a guy twice outside a club. I stabbed him twice in the back, I pinned him to the floor, and I started to cut his ear off. I didn't want to kill him but I needed to teach him a lesson – that's the sort of thing that I was doing then. But a voice called out to me to stop. And I got up – there was a crowd as big as what's here tonight – the crowd parted, I got in my car and drove off. Looking back, I now know that God was speaking to me.

'My heart ballooned, as I said, and a doctor told me that I was going to die. My addiction was killing me – just like it had killed my nine friends. As I keep telling you, my life was over ten years ago. My wife said I needed help and pointed me in the direction of a counsellor, who happened to be a Christian. Now ten years ago I didn't think too much of Christians. I thought they were wimps.

'I went to see this Christian guy because I didn't think he'd be too much trouble to me. I was a guy with a bit of street cred – I could look after myself and I knew always to protect myself – so I still took the knife with me. But he said to me one thing, as I left him, and it hit me between the eyes. He said "You need to choose."

'Ten years ago, I stood in a freezing cold car park, in the East End of London. On my own – not in a church, not with a minister – and I asked God to come into my life. There was no booming voice, no opening of the heavens, no choirs of angels. But something happened. Because for the first time in years, the paranoia went from my life. For the first time in years, fear went from my life. I became a born-again Christian.

'Whether you choose to believe me is irrelevant. But no one can argue the truth of my life. Since I invited Jesus Christ into my life he healed me – he healed my swollen heart. He healed my marriage. He gave me back a life. And I'm competing again – I'm lifting weights and I'm a champion again.

'There are not many Christian sayings that I like. But you know at the age of forty-one, my life was over, and I was "born again". You may not understand that, some of you young people – you've got a long way to go to catch me up. But I'm telling you, to be born again is the greatest feeling I've ever had. I've won many trophies in my time but I'd give them all up. I've never known such a feeling as being filled with the Holy Spirit.

'If anybody tells you that being a Christian is going to make your life rosy then they're not telling you the truth. But I would not go back to the life that I once had. I believe it takes a stronger man to follow Jesus Christ than it does to run from him. And I believe that as a Christian, I'm a bigger man today than I ever was before. Thanks for listening.'

The audience was stunned. Even though I'd been talking through a translator, they had clearly been affected by this story of a man so similar to them. There were many in that crowd who would have known exactly what I was talking about when I spoke of drug addiction, violence and the loss of everything dear to me. They'd been through it themselves. Some of them wanted to see if God could give them the same way out that he gave me.

The shocked silence subsided, and the prisoners began to applaud, then roar their approval.

'Ar-tor! Ar-tor!'

The guards led me back out to the gate; my time inside was up. As I stood outside, in biting cold and falling snow, I wondered again how I ever ended up here. I said a quiet prayer of thanks, got into the waiting car, and took a look at my itinerary for the rest of the week. One prison visited, two to go. I still had plenty of work to do.